*Hold your hour
and have another*

BRENDAN BEHAN

*

Hold your hour and have another

*

Decorations by

BEATRICE BEHAN

HUTCHINSON
London Melbourne Sydney Auckland Johannesburg

Hutchinson & Co. (Publishers) Ltd

An imprint of the Hutchinson Publishing Group

17–21 Conway Street, London W1P 6JD

Hutchinson Publishing Group (Australia) Pty Ltd
16–22 Church Street, Hawthorn, Melbourne, Victoria 3122,
Australia

Hutchinson Group (NZ) Ltd
32–34 View Road, PO Box 40-086, Glenfield, Auckland 10

Huthinson Group (SA) Pty Ltd
PO Box 337, Bergvlei 2012, South Africa

First published 1963
First published as a Hutchinson Paperback 1985
© Brendan Behan 1963
Decorations © Beatrice Behan 1963

Printed and bound in Great Britain
by Anchor Brendon Ltd,
Tiptree, Essex

ISBN 0 09 160311 0

Contents

*

CONTENTS

Acknowledgements

THE ARTICLES collected in this book first appeared in *The Irish Press*. The author is grateful to the editor for giving permission for them to appear in book form.

Do mo Bh.

A seat on the Throne

*

I KNEW A MAN from Nicholas Street that sat on the Throne of England.

He was working for a painting contractor at the time, and must have occupied the royal seat six times a week at least.

'At every tea-break in the morning,' said the Drummer: 'at lunch-time, of course, we went out for beer.'

They were doing up Buckingham Palace at the time, and the tea was made in the usual way, in a billy-can stuck over a blow-lamp.

The Drummer sat up on the Throne because it was the handiest way of looking out into the yard, and keeping an eye out for an approaching foreman.

The Family were not in residence at the time, though this did not prevent unscrupulous persons—a plasterer's helper and a decadent scaffolder—from selling to elderly females in the pub nearby what purported to be bottles of Their Bathwater.

'Some of them just kept it in a bottle and looked at it,' said the Drummer, 'and there was a gentleman that bought the full of a bird-bath off them for three pints of bitter an' a pork pie. He wanted to give his budgie a dip in it for a birthday treat.'

But his finest hour was yet to come when They were returned from Their holidays. The Drummer was painting the flats and risers of a stairs leading to Their private apartments when it happened.

Her Majesty came noiselessly down the stairs and was beside him ere he knew it.

He was still bent over his work, in a kneeling position, and his head bowed devotedly as he coated the current riser.

Then a small and beautifully encased foot nudged him in the ribs, in the region of the paper-brush pocket.

In surprise he glanced up, and tried to rise, in great confusion. 'Your Majesty, I'm so sorry, I——'

But she only smiled graciously and in soothing tones remarked: 'Don't stir, Drummer. I'll step over you.'

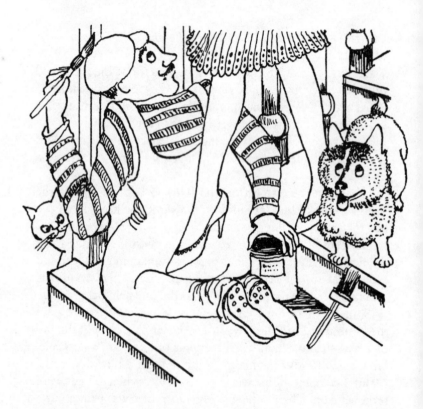

'And when we left,' said the Drummer, 'every man got a hundred box of three greetings cigarettes.'

'There were three greetings on them?'

'There was three wrappings. Like this way. The company
that made them would issue them for Christmas, and they'd
have holly and ivy and Santy Clauseses and log fires and "A
Happy Christmas" on the label. But then say Christmas
passed, and they weren't got rid of, well, the people giving
them could tear off the first label and underneath was another
one, with little yellow chickens, and "A Happy Easter" on
it, and if you didn't get rid of them then, you'd tear off that
label and underneath was a notice saying, "They're getting
stale, you'd better smoke them yourself." '

A small man drinking a fill-up for himself nodded in agree-
ment. 'They gave us them, too, in the Palace.'

'Were you there, too?'

' "Deed and I was,' said little fill-up, 'at sympathy concerts.'

'You were playing at these concerts?' I asked him.

'I don't know whether he was or not,' muttered the
Drummer.

'I didn't say yet whether I was or not,' said little fill-up,
'I only said I was at the sympathy concerts. If yous want to
know, I was in charge of the music mule attached to the
sympathy orchestra for carrying the instruments; in particular
a most unhuman big drum.'

'You weren't playing?'

'No, I had me work cut out trying to soothe the mule, and
he outside nearly going mad from the noise of Beethoven's
Fifth. Just as well if it had have been last, I often thought, and
me struggling to keep Grace Darling—that was the mule's name
on account of his being so vicious—(a joke, if yous folly me)
from going wild round the Palace grounds, and we waiting
to carry the instruments back. Then there was Mozart; there's
a fellow come on a lot since.'

'Them was nice goings-on,' said a snarly-looking customer,
'smoking cigarettes and drinking tea on the Royal Throne of
England and playing music, and the dead dying in dozens for
Ireland every minute of the day. Them was nice things; oh,
Mother Eire, you're rearing them yet.'

He strangled his utterance on a sob and bowed his shoulders on the counter.

'Ah, don't take it too much to heart,' said little fill-up, 'I told you, I only guided the mule.'

'Well,' said the Drummer, 'it was all aiqual to me whose ceiling I whitened. I'd wash off a stretch for the Sheik of Arabee, once he paid the rate.'

Overheard in a bookshop

★

'COULD I HAVE a Dinneen?'[1] asked this respectable-looking party in the bookshop.

'No, sir, we wouldn't have such a thing,' answered the lady assistant. 'I don't know would you get one in Dublin at all. Ectu-ahly,' she finished, 'it's a kind of Cork hoarze doovray,[2] isn't it?'

Your man went off in some puzzlement, and the lady assistant remarked to her young man, elegantly: 'Coming up here and the mark of the stir-about spoon still in their mouth, and looking for them things in a bookshop. You could easy see it was not a pork butcher's. But maybe he thinks it's like the shops back home in the bog where they sell you *Old Moore's Almanac* and a pound of black and white pudding off the one counter.'

Her young man murmured something appropriate, and continued to gaze into her eyes, long and pleadingly. She returned to their own conversation and shook her head for the fourth or fifth time.

'Ignayzeous, I'm really very, very sorry, but I deffiny could not make it. Genuine, I couldn't,' she sighed, 'not but what I'd a loved to.'

An old gentleman came up to ask for a New Testament.

---

[1] *English-Irish Dictionary* compiled by the Reverend Patrick Dinneen, s.j.
[2] *Hors d'œuvres:* in County Cork a favourite snack is a 'drisheen'—a sausage made from dried blood.

'Desperate sorry, I am, sir,' said Ida Lufftoo, 'but I am afraid it's not out yet. We have the old one of course, but I suppose you've read that.'

The old gent looked at her in some dismay and retreated towards the door.

'Cheek and imperance of them old fellows when you go to give them a peas of information. Another fellow comes to me yesterday, a Northern by the sound of him, and he asks for a book about gorilla dazes in Ireland.[1] I told him I'd never seen gorillas dazed, or any other way, in Ireland. Maybe they have them in Ulster, but if so, I said, that was the place to keep them. Then another pair comes in, Yanks they were be the sound of them, and ask me did I know Joyce is useless. I told them I didn't care whether he was or not, not knowing the man, T.G. One fellow has the common gall to laugh up into my face and tell me that was the sharpest crack he'd heard from a European.

' "Go 'way, you dirty low cur," said I, "to insult a lady. I'm no European, but an Irish girl, bred, born and reared in Donnelly's Orchard." '

Her young man muttered something fierce, but she waved her hand deprecatingly.

'That's all right, Ignayzeous, what you'd a done if you'd a been here, but you're like the *Garda Seo Caughtyeh*,[2] never where you're wanted. Then another fellow comes in and asks me for the new Greene, and I directed him to the top of Grafton Street and said he might do the best he could with the old one, because it was the only one I'd heard of in these parts, unless they'd have a new green in Ballyfermot or Donnycarney, out at the new houses, but I'd not know much about them places—ours is a purchase house, fifty pound down and you own it in 2006, if God spares us.

'Then there was an old chap in a Teddy Boy suit, velvet collar and all, drainpipes, and I don't know who he thought he was fooling. Going round in that get-up like a fellow of

[1] *Guerilla Days in Ireland* by Tom Barry.
[2] *An Gárda Síochána*: The Irish Police Force.

eighteen and I declare he was seventy if he was an hour, and he tries to get off his mark, if you please, asking me if I liked Kipling.

' "How could I know?" I asks, "when I never kippilled, and if I did it would be someone more me equals than you."

'And that put him in his place, I can tell you. He wasn't long clearing off. And all these dead-and-alive old books, you'd be lost for a bit of a read only I do bring me *True Romances* with me. I'll be out of this place after the Christmas rush, anyway. I went back to the fellow in the Labour and he says to me: "I thought you *liked* working in a bookshop? You said you worked in one for three years."

' "A bookshop?" says I. "I told you I worked in the cook shop, in the biscuit factory, where they fill cakes and biscuits with jam and suchlike when they come out of the bakehouse."

' "Oh, is that so?" says he. "My mistake; well, keep your mouth shut till the first week in January and let on you can read and write."

' "You're desperate funny, you are," says I. "You're that sharp you'll cut yourself. I can read as good as you," and I read him a real high-class bit out of a book I borrowed here— the real classical, it is, all knowledge, and I read him a bit that stuck him to the ground.

' "Ah, my precious little girl, for God's sake cast occasionally a word or look of encouragement from your velvety lips or saddened eyes! Don't, my treasured hope, don't allow the slightest frown ever formed by the merest movement of Nature to dwell on your sinless brow, else I die. Yes, by Venus; ere I'd yield to have you torn from my arms of life-long companionship, I'd resign my rights of existence to a region of undying flame." '

She put down her book, and smiled gently at Ignayzeous's praises.

A tall lady of foreign, almost diplomatic appearance approached, and with an apologetic smile asked Ida if the Everyman edition of *Anna Karenina* was in stock.

Ida smiled back, interrogatively. 'Urm? Annakarra urm?'

'Tolstoy's *Anna Karenina*,' said the lady.

Ida nodded mysteriously and smiled her inscrutable smile. '*An bhfuil cead agam dul amach?*'[1] she asked.

The lady looked at her and at Ignayzeous, and said, 'Quite—er—thank you.'

Ida's gaze followed her up the shop. 'It doesn't do to let yourself down before these foreigners. When they speak to me in their language I believe in answering them in mine.'

Then her eye took me in. 'Just a minute, Ignayzeous.' To me: 'Did you want to buy something?'

'Well, I was just having a look around,' said I. 'I was just——'

She gently but firmly removed the volume from my lifeless

[1] 'May I go outside?'

fingers and smiled but shook her head. 'Sorry, but no free reads.'

I nodded desperately and turned in the direction of the door, her voice trailing after me.

'I may be only here for a week, Ignayzeous, but I don't want the shop robbed *barefaced*!'

Let's go to town

*

IF YOU DON'T get up and get down town you'd hear nothing, nor find out what they're saying about you. And God send, they're saying something. Good or bad, it's better to be criticized than ignored.

And it was such a fine fresh mild morning that even I was tempted out in the air. From the highlands of Kimmage you could see the mists rising off the city, and the sky rosy and pink out over the head of Howth. The time was seven o'clock, and if Roger Bannister could manage the mile in four minutes, I could get from Sundrive Road to a stationer's in Dame Street in two and a half hours.

I could and did, and had time over for a word with a friend outside the Irish House, at the bottom of Michael's Hill or Winetavern Street. Have it your own way.

Dressed in his sober black, and carrying a small black box, he rubbed his white moustache in greeting.

'You must have had a bad way of lying. It's not eight o'clock yet.'

'I rambled down from the house. I thought the walk would do me good. It's what you'd call close, though I'm sweating.'

'I'm going off to wash off a ceiling for an old one in Foxrock. "Lot of dirt in this room, painter," she says to me yesterday. "I didn't bring any of it with me, ma'am," says I.

'I've a second stock out with me. I don't suppose you'd care to come out and give us a hand?'

I shuddered. I'm allergic to stockbrushes and afraid of knives. Putty knives, hacking knives, and glazing knives.

'Well, I only asked. And you're sweating.'

I wiped my brow.

'You should save that, Brendan. There'd be a cure in that.'

'It's a bit early to be getting the Foxrock people out of bed. What about moseying over as far as the Market and see how the fish and fruit and all to that effect are going on?'

'I suppose we might do worse. I could do with a rossiner myself.'

In Michael's they were listening to the radio, and only took their attention from it to greet us.

There was Mrs. Brennan, and she and I know all belonging to each other from the time of the Invincibles, though her way of talking is infectious and I keep calling her 'Mrs. Brenning'.

She comes down to deal and get her stuff out and on the road, as she's done this sixty years; though nowadays she directs operations from a seat in the corner, and children and grandchildren keep running in and out to get her directions on the price of this and who's to take what go-car of fish, fruit, or vegetables, where.

And Crippen, who has resigned from active participation in the great world of commerce and industry, and is by way of being a literary man to the extent of writing three cross-doubles for the female clientele of the bookies up the street. He also had a connection with a well-known literary journal, as a broker in International Reply Coupons, which he changed in the bookies'.

'So your man is in London, eh?'

'A shocking lot in Londing,' says Mrs. Brennan to her friend beside her, in the corner.

'Ah,' says Crippen, casually, 'it's an editor we used to know.'

'An editor,' murmurs Mrs. Brennan to her friend, impressively. 'Mind that, now. If Mr. Cripping and Mr. Behing didn't go to school, they met the scholars coming back. It's all the educayshing.'

'Well,' smiled Crippen, modestly. 'I dare swear I could make out the odds to a hundred-to-eight shot as good as the next. 'Course this man was a Varsity man. National and Trinity and all to that effect.'

'Look at that now, Maria. In the Natural Trimity College.'

'He's on the Third Programme now,' said I.

'And the same fellow,' said Crippen. 'He could be on the First if he only minded himself.'

'And where do you leave Brending Behing, there, beside you? Took second prize of ten shillings or six pound of fresh beef at the Carnival in Mountjoy Square. Saw him myself. Not today nor yesterday. Playing the mouth-orging.'

She looked at my friend, the painter.

'It was in aid of the new hall in Phibsboro. Near Daly-mount.'

'I know it up there,' said the painter. 'I worked in a presbytery not far from it. Grained and varnished the priests' desks.'

'Look at that now, Maria, what the man did. Vanished the priests' destes. You'll have luck with it, sir.'

'And I should be on my way out to a bit this morning.'

'Ah, hold your hour and have another. You should take Brending with you and get his weight down. I heard he gets his clothes made in the Hammongd Laying Fouingdry[1] these times.'

'Just wait till you hear a bit of this on the wireless. It's shocking funny.'

'That's right,' said Crippen, 'turn it up there, Michael, till we get another bit. It's better nor horse opera.'

'He talks massive,' said Mrs. Brennan, 'you have to give him that.'

'. . . and I'm glad to see they are all well muffled up, as they walk towards the quayside. This cold morning air can be quite sharp . . .'

'I'd have sent over the loan of me shawl if I'd a known,' muttered Maria.

'. . . and they are, yes, they are, I'm sure they are shivering, though ever so slightly; this morning air from the sea, and a swell is rocking the vessel ever so slightly . . .'

'The cheek of it.'

'. . . and I really think that they are, in actual fact, I'm sure they have, or are going to, if they have not already, but I must really, now, pass you to my friend Redmond . . .'

'. . . thank YOU, Cedric Hall-Ball, and now, briefly to recapitulate the journey out, some months ago, was the first they had flown in an aeroplane . . .'

'They usually flew in a wheelbarrow,' said Crippen.

'All the same,' said Mrs. Brennan, 'it's a bit of gas, and I like to start the day with a bit of laugh. Good morning, all. We've to go up as far as Candem Street.'

'We'll be out with you,' said the painter. 'I've to start out for this old one's ceiling in Foxrock.'

'And I've to buy a new ribbon for the old Remington.'

'Mark that judiciously, Maria,' said Mrs. Brennan, 'he's to buy a new ribbon for his Renningtom.'

---

[1] Hammond Lane, a Dublin foundry.

A turn for a neighbour

*

ONE CHRISTMAS EVE, though not this one nor the one before, there was a man coming in from Cloghran, County Dublin, on a horse and cart to do his Christmas business, selling and buying.

When he got as far as Santry, County Dublin, he remembered that there was an old neighbour dead in a house, so he went in to pay his respects, and after saying that he was sorry for their trouble, and all to that effect, he enquired whether he could offer any assistance of a practical nature.

'Well, if it's a thing you wouldn't mind, collecting the coffin; it's ready-measured and made and all; it would be a great help to us.'

'I do not indeed mind carrying the coffin back for you, though I won't be home till a bit late, having to do her shopping. I've a list as long as your arm, of sweets for children, snuff for her old one, rich cake, a jar of malt, two bottles of port wine, snuff for my old one, a collar for the dog, a big red candle to put in the window, a jockey of tobacco for myself, a firkin of porter, two dolls that'll say "Ma-Ma", one railway train, a jack-in-the-box and a monkey-on-a-stick, two holy pictures, rashers, and black and white pudding and various other combustibles too numerous to mention.

'But I'll stick the coffin up amongst the rest of them, and take the height of good care of it, and it'll be me Christmas box and hansel for me poor old neighbour and a good turn for myself because I'll have luck with it.'

So off he went at a jog-trot into the city down from Santry, County Dublin, past Ellenfield and Larkhill, through the big high trees, and the sun just beginning on a feeble attempt to come out, and then having a look at the weather it was in, losing heart, and going back in again, till your man came to Whitehall tram terminus, where they were just getting ready to take the seven o'clock into town.

'Morra, Mick,' shouts a tram fellow, with his mouth full of steam; 'and how's the form?'

'If it was any better,' shouts Mick off the cart, 'I couldn't stick it.'

'More of that to you,' shouts the tram fellow, 'and a happy Christmas, what's more.'

'You, too, and may more along with that,' shouts Mick, and along with him down the Drumcondra Road.

So away he goes into the city, over Binn's Bridge, and into the markets. Before dinner-time he had his selling done and was on to the buying.

He had a good few places to visit, meeting this one and that, but with an odd adjournment he had everything bought and the coffin collected and on the back of the cart with the rest of the stuff by evening-time. It was dark and cold and the snow starting to come down the back of his neck, but he tightened the collar well round him, and having plenty of the right stuff inside him began a bar of a song for himself, to the tune of *Haste to the Wedding*:

' 'Twas beyond at Mick Reddin's, at Owen Doyle's weddin,
  The lads got the pair of us out for a reel,
    Says I, "Boys, excuse us," says they, "don't refuse us,"
  "I'll play nice and aisy," said Larry O'Neill.

Then up we got leppin' it, kickin' and steppin' it,
  Herself and myself on the back of the door,
    Till Molly, God bless her, fell into the dresser,
  And I tumbled over a child on the floor.

'Says herself to myself, "You're as good as the rest,"
Says myself to herself, "Sure you're better nor gold."
Says herself to myself, "We're as good as the best of them,"
"Girl," says I, "sure we're time enough old." '

So, with a bit of a song and a mutter of encouragement to
the old horse, Mick shortened the way for himself, through
snow and dark, till he came to Santry, County Dublin, once
again.

There was light and smoke and the sound of glasses and some
fellow singing the song of *The Bould Tenant Farmer*, and Mick,
being only human, decided to make one last call and pay his
respects to the publican.

But getting in was a bit easier than getting out, with drinks
coming up from a crowd that was over from the other side of
the county, all Doyles, from the hill of Kilmashogue, the
Drummer Doyle, the Dandy Doyle, Jowls Doyle, Woodener
Doyle, the Dancer Doyle, Elbow Doyle, Altarboy Doyle, the
Hatchet Doyle, Coddle Doyle, the Rebel Doyle, Uncle Doyle,
the Shepherd Doyle, Hurrah Doyle and Porternose Doyle.

There was singing and wound opening, and citizens dying
for their country on all sides, and who shot the nigger on the
Naas Road, and I'm the first man that stuck a monkey in a
dustbin and came out without a scratch and there's a man
there will prove it, that the lie may choke me, and me country's
up and me blood is in me knuckles. 'I don't care a curse now
for you, or your queen, but I'll stand by my colour, the harp
and the green.'

Till by the time he got on the road again Mick was *maith-go-
leor*,[1] as the man said, but everything went well till he was
getting near Cloghran and he had a look round, and there he
noticed—the coffin was gone! Gone, like Lord Norbury with
the divil, as the man said.

Ah, what could he do at all, at all? He sat on the cart for a
minute and wondered how he'd face your man if he had to go

[1] Good enough.

and tell him that he'd let him down not doing the turn for a family with enough of trouble this Christmas Eve.

Still, looking at it never fattened the pig, so he got off and went back along the road in the direction of the city, and was moseying round in the snow when an R.I.C.[1] man came up from Santry Barracks.

'Come on you, now, and what are you doing walking round this hour of the night?'

'I'm after losing a coffin, constable,' says Mick.

'They sells desperate bad stuff this time of the year,' sighs the policeman, taking Mick by the arm. 'Come on, my good man, you'll have to come down the road with me now till we instigate investigations into your moves.'

Poor Mick was too disheartened even to resist him, and, sad and sober, he trudged through the snow till they came to the barracks. They went into the dayroom and the constable

[1] Royal Irish Constabulary.

said to the sergeant, 'I've a fellow here, wandering abroad, and says he's after losing a coffin.'

'He may well have,' says the sergeant, 'because we're after finding one. There it is, standing up behind the door.'

They looked round and Mick's face lit up with joy and relief. 'Praise Him,' said he, running over and throwing his arms round it, 'there it is, me lovely coffin.'

He explained all about it, and they let him go off carrying it back to the cart.

'Take better care of it, now,' says the constable and the sergeant from the door.

'I wouldn't have minded,' says Mick, 'only this coffin is not my own. Good night and a happy Christmas to you, and to everyone.'

Music by Suffering Ducks

*

'What is your occupation?' the judge asked the Hop Connell.

'I'm a Suffering Duck, your warship,' said the Hop.

So he was, too. He played the oboe in it. The Unemployed Band was its official name, and they were in court due to a suspected incitement to a breach of the peace.

It was during the 1913 strike when they serenaded the Royal Irish inhabitants of Fitzgibbon Street Barracks with the endearing strains of *The Peeler and the Goat*, and followed a marching column of police with the lively tune *Here's the Robbers Passing By*, in step with these stalwarts of the force proceeding on their majestic, imperial way to O'Connell Street.

'You call it a band of musicians,' said the magistrate, 'I call it a band of hooligans.'

But there was such a roar from the thousands of other hooligans round the court that he decided that the Pax Britannica was best served by letting them off with a caution, when the band marched off triumphantly playing the loyal air *The British Grenadiers*, to the special lyrics of their supporters, who roared the chorus all the way back up through Parnell Street and Summerhill:

'The Boers they were marching and the British wanted fight,
The Boers fired their rifles and blew them out of sight,
Sound the bugle, sound the drum,
Three cheers for ould Paul Kruger . . .'

The Hop led the parade to the North Circular Road, where the proceedings were adjourned to the corner shop, for there's not many a musician but likes having his whistle moistened or his bow rosined.

The only notable exception was James Whiteside, the 'Bard of Bray', who played the harp, the pipes, and the fiddle and composed the following song:

Sobriety is making way in the Ireland of today,
Fill the bumper fair, every drop is poison,
Will you walk into my parlour, said the spider to the fly,
'Tis the prettiest little drunkery that ever you did spy,
Oh, join the abstainers and you'll be the gainers . . .

James, like Bach, another notable musician, is no longer composing, but decomposing this many a long year. I am bound to state however, that there is no discredit to his teetotal habits, as he was born in 1844 and no engine, no matter how well oiled, can be expected to go on for ever.

The aforementioned Hop was one of a number of Republican musicians I knew in my childhood. They were friends of my father and of my uncle, both of whom were very good fiddlers.

I heard of two fine musicians in the years immediately after the Civil War kept out of their jobs by the oath of allegiance, and playing the violin in Rathmines for pennies. Unfortunately, through embarrassment they kept to the back streets and didn't get much. They often told me about it since, over a 'bumper fair' in a comfortable lounge, I'm glad to say. We live through the winter and the divil would not kill us in summer.

Someone said of the bagpipes that the best thing about them was the fact that they didn't smell too, but what foot could keep easy when the pipes were screeching *Allistrums's March*, *O'Neill's*, or *The Brian Boru*?

I heard the East Belfast come down the Shankill on the Twelfth playing *Rosc Catha na Mumhan* disguised as the *Boyne Water*, and be damn but I nearly fell in behind them and their King Billy banner.

It would make the dead walk even to hear the names of the tunes the Uileann pipers played—*Give me your hand*, *The unfortunate cup of tea*, *Young Roger was a ploughboy* (I know the words of that, too), *Upstairs in a tent*, *Larry Grogan*, *The Cronán Gabhair*, and where do you leave the flower of Irish music, *The Coulin*? It was the tune Commandant Reggie Dunne played on the fiddle the night before he was hanged in Pentonville with his comrade Volunteer Joe O'Sullivan, and it is part of the London-Irish tradition for Frank Lee to play it on the organ in Maiden Lane after their annual Mass.

I often heard it told how the Hop Connell got a hold of a tin whistle somewhere on the way to Frongoch and struck up

O Donnell Abu, and lifted the tired feet of his comrades into a defiant tramp to captivity. Not that he was much in the marching line himself.

'I see,' said a British officer, looking down at the musicians, 'they have cripples in their army.'

The Hop removed the tin whistle from his mouth. 'We have,' said he, 'but no conscripts.'

Up the ballad-singers

*

'An' sure, if he spent it on mountainy dew,
I'd sooner he drank it, nor gev it to you,
Your lavins of bailiffs should be hung from a yew–
Tree,' says the wife of the Bould Tenant Farmer.

I HEARD this good song from an old County Dublin man, in
the Wran's Nest, out in the Strawberry Beds, last summer, and
it goes to the air of *Fágaimid Siúd mar atá Sé*.[1]

I write 'an'' instead of 'and', and 'gev' and 'lavins' instead
of 'gave' and 'leavings', because that was how the man
pronounced it. I write 'Wran's Nest', instead of 'Wren's Nest',
for the same reason; in case you think I don't know any better.

According to some nationally minded citizens, it would be
as much as your life is worth to even hint that the English-
speaking Gael hasn't got the same way of speaking as the
B.B.C. or Oxford University. The same nationally minded
citizens practically killed the old ballads of Dublin forty years
ago with the rise of the Gaelic League.

My mother could sing *Casadh an tSugáin*,[2] and a lovely song
it is, but her generation were made ashamed of the old tunes
that kept up the hearts of the people for years, and it was only
because I was curious, and still am, to find out what they used
to sing in the times before herself and other good people picked
up a bit of Irish, and because I made a point of listening to the

[1] *We'll leave it so, as it is.*
[2] *The Twisting of the Rope.*

31

old songs from the unregenerate pre-Gaelic League people, that I know them.

I often heard it regretted that most of the people in the country parts lost the language, in one generation removed from the older people of now, but surely it was some loss that the people of the period of 'sixteen and after were told that the old songs of the Northside and the Liberties were 'stage-Irish', 'coarse', 'made a show of the country', and were made ashamed of the old songs to such an extent, that even the sad and lovely *Kevin Barry*, known and sung the two sides of the Irish Sea and the Atlantic, has been, all its life, an outlaw from any Dublin hooley.

Even poor old Tom Moore's songs were only remembered because they could not forget them. I am prepared to admit that the words of *The Last Rose of Summer* are not as good as those of *Jimmy, mo mhile stór*,[1] to the original Gaelic air; but the music is, even in its dolled-up drawing-room style, a bit above the level of the air they put to Mangan's *Dark Rosaleen*, and the song was considered by Flotow good enough for insertion into the opera *Martha*.

The most ardent pikemen songsters felt a little squeamish about the so-called Park Murders, and it is to the ballad-makers of the Hidden Ireland of the slums that we are indebted for songs about the Invincibles. They never got into the books.

One of the best of them came from the Falls Road and it was from a man of the Pound Loanie that I heard it, to the air of the *Crúiscín Lán*:[2]

'Get up,' says Skin-the-Goat, 'and I'll drive you to the boat.'

and,

James Carey with his son, to the Castle they did run,
But Number One was gone, boys, gone. . . .

Alas, that's all I remember of it.

[1] *Jimmy, my thousand treasures.*
[2] *My Full Little Jug;* a seventeenth-century drinking-song.

But the best one can be heard nearly any morning round the markets from the old ones, with a bit, or drop, of prompting:

I am a bold undaunted youth, Joe Brady is my name,
From the chapel of North Anne Street one Sunday as I came,
All to my surprise who should I espy but Moreno and Cockade;[1]
Says one unto the other: 'Here comes our Fenian blade.'

Though they weren't above looting a tune or so from the

[1] Detectives.

London musical shows, when it suited their own suave and savage humour, in the Tan time:

Oh, never marry a soldier, a sailor or a Marine,
If you can get a rebel in his uniform of green.
How right you are. . . .
The Boers put them in khaki, the Germans beat them black
    and blue,
But the boys put them in cages, like the monkeys at the zoo.
How right you are, how right you are. . . .

I was told by Mrs. Dolan, a rebel and the mother of rebels—from Percy Street, Ton Street, or Durham Street off the Falls Road, I can never remember which—that in the pogroms the people used to warn one another of the approach of the murder gang, from street to street, by rattling the tops of the dustbins, which would drum with an ever-increasing din that could be heard all over Belfast and give rise to the song:

Come out and rattle your bin,
Tiddy-fol-loll, tiddy-fol-lay.

In the Boyne Tavern in the Shankill, I was called upon for a song myself, and, as cute as a Christian, what do you think I sang? *Put More Turf on the Fire, Mary Anne.* Discretion was the better part of valour. Though the company were decent Protestant workers, you never know what half-fool is lying in the background waiting to make a name for himself by crowning the stranger with a porter bottle—you get them everywhere.

For the matter of that, it was a Protestant navvy, Sean O'Casey, who wrote one of the master anti-recruiting songs of the 1914–18 war:

'Come on, you land of saints and bards,'
Says the Grand Ould Dame Britannia.
'Will yous come and join the Irish Guards?'
Says the Grand Ould Dame Britannia.

I'm a British Object, said the Belfast-Man

★

'I'M A BRITISH OBJECT,' said this elderly Belfast-man to me, one Twelfth of July, a long time ago. We were in the little village of Millisle, near Donaghadee in the County Down. We had gone out there to pass the beautiful day of high summer like true Irishmen, locked in the dark snug of a public house.

The Belfast-man was an inebriate of some standing, whose politics were purely alcoholic. He was what they call in the North-East a wine victim, and carried his affection for things British to drinking port from the vineyards of Hoxton, and sherry from Tooting Bec, at five shillings the ten-glass bottle. He had come down for the day from the city and scandalized the assembled Orangemen by his reluctance to drink porter.

That lovely summer's day I'll remember too for the singing of an old man from Millisle. *The Bright Silvery Light of the Moon* and the *Yellow Rose of Texas* he sang, and disappointed me because he didn't sing something more Orange. The nearest he got to 'party politics' was a song about the Crimean War that went to the air of *The Rakes of Mallow*:

> All drawn up, Britannia's sons
> Faced the Russian tyrant's guns,
> And bravely dared his shells and bombs,
> On the Bonny Heights of Alma.

We had a great day of singing and drinking and eating, and though I did feel a bit shamed by the bright sunshine when we came out blinking into it at closing-time, it wasn't long before we got indoors again.

Next morning I didn't feel so good, but in the summer-time nothing lasts long, and I was swimming around the harbour like a two-year-old and was shortly joined by a young man from the Shankill, who confided in me that he could always 'tell a Fenian'.

'And how,' said I, lying on the sea, *bolg anairde*,[1] and looking up at the sun, 'do you manage that?'

'Ah know them be their wee button noses.'

I felt my own snitcher, and reflected that it would make a peculiar surrealistic sort of wee button.

The British Object was not so politically unaware as I'd thought. He too appeared, ready for the waves, dressed in a

[1] Belly upwards.

high-necked black costume that bore some resemblance to a habit, and emblazoned with an enormous orange crest with the inscription 'True to You', and surmounted not as you might expect by a ten-glass bottle of Liverpool champagne, but by a head of the late King Edward the Seventh.

He dived in and thrashed about like a man in the jigs, and I confidently expected the sea to become wine-coloured after him, like 'the wine-coloured ocean' of Homer.

I'd not have believed a person if they'd told me that summer would ever end, or I'd have believed them as one believes a mathematical proposition, from the mind out only.

It seems years ago since the summer when we were crowded jam-tight from Merrion to Seapoint, and half doped from the sun when the pavements of Grafton Street were like the top of an oven, and you had to dodge into Mac's and get yourself on the high stool for the safety of the soles of your feet.

Is it only a short time ago that I stood at ten o'clock of an evening in the little town of Callan, and went over to read the inscription over the house of Humphrey O'Sullivan, the Gaelic diarist and poet, now most appropriately a fish-and-chip shop?

Poets are great one-and-one men. I don't know about diarists.

I'd sample the chips another time, with a bit of ray, but that evening I had eaten at Mrs. Coady's, and after her huge rounds of prime beef and fresh vegetables you wouldn't be in humour of anything for a good while.

I'd come out from her place trying to remember the name, and getting mixed up, muttering in a daze of good living, like an incantation, charm or spell, the words 'Mrs. Callan of Coady', I mean 'Mrs. Coady of Callan'.

And the Guard I met, that told me of raiding a pub after hours and finding three men in it. And the publican starts 'ah-sure-ing' him that they're only friends that he wants to give a farewell drink to, because they're off to Lourdes the following day.

The Guard says all right, and not be too long and, going out, meets three others on their way to the hall door.

Regretting his previous mildness, he enquires sarcastically: 'And I suppose you three are going to Lourdes, too?'

'Musha no, sergeant, *a mhic*, we're going to Knock.'[1]

[1] Knock: a place of Irish pilgrimage.

Happy birthday to you

*

IN OUR STREET general indignation was stirred by the case of Jack versus *Saorstat Eireann*,[1] consequent upon Jack being put off the labour by a hatch clerk, who had seen him march on the Gaiety stage as an Austro-Hungarian infantryman in the second act of *The Student Prince*. The hatch clerk, having seen him sign on that morning as an unemployed person, made a report and Jack's dole was stopped.

'I told him,' said Jack, 'that I was only appearing for the sake of art and the chance of lifting a white silk shirt, which as an Imperial Blaggard I wore as part of me get-up; but it was no use; he said it was employment within the meaning of the act, and me dole is stopped, and I'm being had up in Number Two Court in the case of Me versus *Saorstat Eireann*.'

'*Sayers Todd Hernon*,' muttered Lime Looney, grimly, 'that Buff—in the law racket now, is he? There's a result. I knew him when he had nothing.

'Was it,' he stood up on his tippy-toes and raised his voice, 'was it for a scruffhound, and I can call him no less, like *Sayers Todd Hernon* to be swearing away the life of Jack?'

'See the Releeving Ovvicer, Jack,' said the Granny Nutty from a corner of the snug. 'I softened his cough.' She smiled reminiscently, or rearranged her wrinkles; the nearest thing to a smile you ever saw.

'The time they tried to stop a day's money on poor ould

[1] The former Irish Free State.

39

Winnie the Witch, because she missed a day's signing due to
the ruffins in the room overhead hanging a sack over her
window, so that she stopped in bed forty-eight hours not
knowing night from day. That's why I'd see. Tell him,' she
simpered, 'tell him I sent you.'

Now, many right-minded people are of the opinion that to
walk on in *The Student Prince* for fifteen shillings a week, while
getting nine shillings a week for signing on as an unemployed
man, and thus making a total of one pound four shillings for a
weekly income, is a great crime.

Most right-minded people, even in 1930, had an income
many times one pound four shillings a week, but there weren't
many of them knocking around our way.

We differed in opinion over some things to an extent of
extreme spikery round about Armistice Day, when a riot was
caused in Jimmy-the-Sports, by an ex-Dublin Fusilier telling
a relative of mine that he had often seen a bigger row over beer
in the canteen of a Saturday night, than a certain Tan war
ambush in which this relative of mine had taken part.

My relative informed him that if he, the Fusilier, had killed
any Germans, they were harmless ones to be killed be the likes
of him that couldn't beat his way out of a paper bag.

But in the matter of Jack Rivers getting a few makes for
walking on the stage in *The Student Prince*, and not losing two
weeks' dole money by telling the labour about his one week's
work, we hadn't enough readies to enable us to meet a just
and moral conclusion—we were all for Jack.

All his fourteen children (even Lollie that was not much
liked, since she clapped Chuckles Cleary on the back when he
was blowing out a mouthful of paraffin oil on a lighted
match) became great heroes, and when we saw the rozzers
march down the road, we ran down the lane with them, to hide
them from *Sayers Todd Hernon*, who, I personally thought, was
a well-dressed gentleman of exceptional ferocity, with apartments in Fitzgibbon Street Barracks and who dined off
children whose fathers weren't working.

Sometimes when they had marched on in the direction of Croke Park, we'd let a shout after them:

'Harvey Duff, don't catch me,
Catch the fellow behind the tree.'

and roar 'Up the Republic'. I wasn't sure why we roared 'Up the Republic', only to annoy the rozzers. I was sure that the Republic had not much time for *Sayers Todd Hernon*.

But before Jack's case came off there was an election, and T.D.'s[1] and would-be T.D.'s of all and every political persuasion were being chased up the North Circular till they promised to 'look into the case'.

They did, and better than that, Jack got a job digging the Circular Road, at the Big Tree at Dorset Street, between Summerhill and the 'Joy'[2] (if you've ever heard of that place),

[1] *Teachta Dála*, Member of Parliament.
[2] Mountjoy Prison.

and arrived there with his pick and shovel as good as the next man.

At half past ten the foreman came up, looked at his watch, and nodded, at which the assembled Gaels bowed their heads low, and united their voices in:

'Happy Birthday to you, happy birthday to you,
Happy Birthday, happy birthday, happy birthday to you . . .'

Jack asked the more experienced Gael beside him whether it was the ganger's birthday.

'No,' says your man, 'but it's the second anniversary of the hole.'

Dialogue on Literature

*

A VOICE (hoarse, relentless): 'Where were you in 'sixteen?'
   'I wasn't born till 'twenty-three.'
   A.V.: 'Excuses . . . always excuses.'
   ('You borrowed that from *Living with Lynch.*' 'I stole it, sir.
An artist never borrows.')
   A mirthless laugh rang through the snug at the far end of
the shop. A shudder ran through me, and I ventured to the
side door to have a look in the mirror, and a better view of the
source of that awful sound (the mirthless laugh, I mean).
   I knew the voice only too well, and the face and all.
   It was the face of the Rasher Cambel, the Dolphin's Barn
genius.
   'Well,' he looked round at me, 'hack.'
   'I was a hack,' says I, 'before you came up.'
   I gazed down at my vis-à-vis, as the man said; he could not
deny it. (At fifty, George Moore learned the comfort of semi-
colons; us National schoolboys picks it up a bit earlier.)
   'My friend, Ma Loney, ah dear heavens,' says the Rasher, in
the one breath and looking very hard at the two fellows out of
the Artists' Fellowship. These were two youths out of the
Corporation, and looked hard at me when he said these words,
'was a liar.'
   'Shut up your big mouth now,' says Mister Moo, as he is
called for short. 'I do not allow that kind of abuse of my
customers, even if they have monthly pensions itself.' He
nodded round, and we nodded.

43

'Mister Moo,' said I, that being short for his name, 'sure I never wrote a book with a hard cover? You're the man that knows that.'

'Bedad and you never did, barring you did between the hours of half-two and half-three.'[1]

'Oh, indeed and he did not,' said Maria Concepta from the corner; 'indeed and he did not ever go in for anythin' so forren as writin' books. Sure that boy, he can't read, never mind write.'

'I don't know whether he did or not,' says the Rasher. 'He attacked in print a friend of mine. One who is not in the common run of—ah-ah-ha——'

'Now, now, "ha-ha" yourself,' said Maria Concepta. 'I'll give you "ha-ha!"'

'He attacked in print,' said the Rasher, impressively, 'a friend of mine, who is not in the common run of ha-ha——'

'Ha-ha is not proper abuse, sir,' said Maria Concepta.

'Ha-hackery,' said the Rasher. 'The man is a hack.'

I shivered my nostrils and whinnied.

'Well, now,' said Crippen, 'he has a look of the quinine speeshes,' and added with elegance, 'when you see under the gate.'

'My friend,' said the Rasher, 'the liar.'

'Ah, no, that's enough,' said Mister Moo.

'I meant, a barrister,' said the Rasher, with dignity.

'I'm sorry, decent man,' said Mister Moo, 'you meant a lawyer; sure no one would have an hour's luck attacking the likes of them fellows; no man of education would attack the like, and I can see you're an Eton man like meself.'

'Aye,' muttered Crippen, 'and a drinkin' man if you went into it.'

'That's not ayther here nor there, now,' said Mister Moo. 'I'm not waiting on the likes of you to tell me that.'

'But, all the same,' said the Rasher, who had been in Soho for some time, 'actually—that person.'

---

[1] The hour in Ireland when the pubs are closed.

'Oh, indeed, now,' said Maria Concepta, 'there's no need for language the like of that. Going round calling people persons. And they not doing a ha'porth on you.'

'The lady's right,' said Mister Moo to the Rasher; 'there's no persons here.'

'No, indeed,' said Maria Concepta, 'we served and seen every class of people here, but no persons.'

'Nevertheless,' screeched the Rasher.

'Oh, nevertheless,' said Maria Concepta, reasonably.

'But very much the more,' said Crippen, sincerely.

'That hack,' said the Rasher, looking straight at me, 'attacked a friend of mine. A friend of humanity's. A real writer—not—' he shouted, defiantly, 'one whose name will be found on the flyleaf of thick volumes, but whose more delicate moods——'

'The same again, men?' asked Mister Moo.

He was waved away.

'But whose happiest sentiments may be found——'

'In the slim sheaf of verse,' murmured Crippen.

The Rasher nodded. 'How did you know, red——'

'Redolent of the faintest faery feylike feeling,' muttered Crippen.

'Genius,' said the Rasher respectfully. 'How did you know?'

'Never mind poor Brending Behing,' said Crippen, 'he doesn't know what he writes.'

'How so?' asked the Rasher.

'Sad case,' said Crippen, looking at me with commiseration. 'Only went to school half the time, when they were teaching the writing—can't read.'

Our budding genius here

*

'I'M SUSPENDED that much, I don't know whether I'm coming or going,' said Mrs. Brennan. 'If only we knew what she was going to do, one way or another, but she'll have to make up her mind about him. I can't stand being suspended any more; can you, Mr. Cripping, sir?'

> 'If we only knew,
> What she was going to do,
> Did she but reach a decision
> And end our surmission.'

quoted Crippen, adding: 'Them lines is be Yeets.' He turned to me. 'I suppose our budding genius here——'

'That's what he is, Mr. Cripping. A pudding cheenis. I knew his poor granny, God be good to her, and she was another, and never used any but white snuff, so she didn't, isn't that right, Maria Concepta?'

'Trew, trew, trew, Mrs. Brenning, ma'am,' croaked Maria Concepta, 'but go on, Mr. Cripping, sir, with the poetery. Carry on with the coffing, the corpse will walk.'

'I was going to ask Behing here, this honorary journalist, whether he was familiar with that poem be Yeets that begins "O, to have a little house".'

'The Scotch House,' muttered Maria Concepta. 'He has you there. Behing here, onrey churnalist, and pudding cheenyuss, you've the shape of wan, anyway, what matter.'

'Maria Concepta, you're rambling that far, you'll be bona fide in a minute,' said Mrs. Brennan. 'Get a grip of yourself be the two hands and pull yourself together.'

'I can't help it, Mrs. Brenning, ma'am. I'm in suspenders over this other one. Will she or won't she?'

'We're all the one way,' said Mrs. Brennan. ' "I ahpreeshy ate your pree dick ah ment," as the gentleming said and him trying to get the hot sassidge outa the coddle,[1] but that's not to say, be the same toking of regard, that we're all to drop down dead of the drewth while she makes up her mind. This is the hour of decishing——'

'Brought to yous each evening be the——'

'Maria Concepta, you're wandering again, what are you having?—that'll bring her to.'

'I'll have a drain of the other, Mrs. Brenning ma'am. Me nerves is gone from the straying.'

'It's a straying on all of us. Michael, will you have the deezensy to stop picking your nose there and do what you're supposed to do be the powers of your special exempting—to wit, supply persons lawfully attending said fair and market with a gargle?'

'All right, all right,' said Michael, 'and no word about him and her yet?'

'Not a word,' said Crippen. 'She's gone away to the country for a few days, I heard.'

'Ah, now, when all is said and done—a little sup of peppermint in that, Michael, ee you pleeze—it's hard on her. I feel it as if it was me daughter,' said Mrs. Brennan. 'Wimming feels for wimming, isn't that right, Maria Concepta?'

'You could sing it, Mrs. Brenning, and play it on a mellowjing if you had an air to it. Wimming feels for wimming—and, of course, when all is said and done, it's for love. I remember my poor fellow, I often told yous, Cripping and Behing, no need to tell Mrs. Brenning there, she knew him well——'

---

[1] A Dublin stew consisting of boiled sausages, rashers and potatoes.

'Is it poor Gobbles, Maria Concepta? Didn't I separate him and me own poor dear deeparted, the night they came out of the hot meat shop in Thomas Court Bawn and went to fight a jewel with a backbone each?'

'I met him, the Lord have mercy on him, and he coming out of the Somali village, the year of the exhibishing. I sees this pig me, as black as your boot, and pouring sweat, though it wasn't for all he was wearing, after doing the war dance of the Mosambongas, and he runs after me with the spear. I screeched mela[1] murders and ran like the hammers of hell, with him after me till he got me in a corner, and I near went in a weakness. I thought of offering him me glass beads from off me neck, but they were a pair I borrowed off me sister, Teasy, and I was more afraid of her; but I looked into his black face, and his eyes rolling in his head, and I moaned and said, "You Zulu," and I was going to say, "Me too," God forgive me, when he

[1] *Míle*: a thousand.

caught me pashing at lee to his heaving boozem, and whispered, "Would you ever go down as far as Searson's for three
glasses of porter in a jug?" '

'Ah, yes, the course of trew love is ever up a hill,' sighed
Mrs. Brennan. 'Mr. Cripping, sir, you have sorceresses of
informayshing; do you think she will or she willn't?'

'I don't know,' said Crippen. 'I heard the clergy say she
shouldn't, and some of the people says she should, and I don't
like this going off to the country for a few days——'

But there was a commotion in the street outside and Mrs.
Brennan dashed out in the middle of his sentence, close followed
by Maria Concepta. Crippen and I were making hurried
efforts to finish our pints when they burst back in the door,
just as quick.

'It's all over,' said Mrs. Brennan, 'she's not going to do it.
I'm nearly weak, so I am.'

'So am I,' muttered Maria Concepta, reaching her hand out
on the counter for a tumbler to grip.

'I'll stand,' said Michael. 'What are yous for?'

Maria Concepta struggled to the door again. 'They're
coming down here—her and him linking her. Here they are.'
In great excitement she held open the door, and in came a
woman with a black eye, followed by a man.

'I couldn't do it in the finish,' said the black-eyed lady. 'Not
when I saw that ould Bridewell. I couldn't charge him; not if
he gave me a black eye in every part of me body—and out in
the country, in the sister's place in East Finglas, I missed him.'

'And I missed her,' muttered your man.

'Maybe she won't miss you the next time with a pot,' said
Mrs. Brennan severely.

'I suppose,' said Crippen, 'it's better to be fighting than to be
lonely.'

I help with the sheep

A WOMAN came to Pádraic Pearse complaining about her son's progress, or lack of it, at school. 'He doesn't seem to want to do anything,' she said. 'I don't see any future for him except playing the tin whistle. What am I to do with him?'

'Buy him a tin whistle,' said Pearse.

In my capacity as shepherd on Timahoe Bog, I stood in the town of Kilcock—'the famous town of Kilcock,' as its inhabitants call it—and listened to the music of some half a school-load of Christian Brothers' boys playing the *Wearing of the Green* and *Fainne Geal an Lae* on their tin whistles.

I hope the young Byrnes and O'Connors will excuse me so describing them. I know that in the school they are described as flageolets, but to us older shams they'd be more readily described as tin whistles.

Anyway, they made very good music with them, whatever you'd want to call them, and I listening next door.

Snug enough I was, too, before they dug me out and went up to the sheep.

Accursed and vicious breed. Nest of vipers. Coy and humorous, if you can call it humour making a man of fourteen stone charge over barbed wire and land to his armpits in the mud of centuries.

You never saw me chasing sheep? You've never lived. I was left in such a state after them that my nearest relative would have felt sorry for me.

The object was to get up to Timahoe Bog, get them

marshalled into some sort of order, and get a hundred of them carted into Prussia Street.

We left Billy's after interrupting a discussion I was having with the man of the house about the practice—which, we agreed, was a disgusting one—of spelling such old words as *Dún Laoghaire*, '*Dún Laoire*', and *céilidhe*, '*céili*'.

I was telling Billy that everyone that had occasion to go there, whether from England or Ireland, knew the port as *Dún Laoghaire*, and that the only one I had ever heard to get himself mixed up with the word '*céilidhe*' was my friend Eddy Chapman, who, on leaving a boat with me at Clyde Quay in Glasgow, told me that he would see me at the Celluloid Bar in an hour's time.

But he, despite the uncompromising Scottish spelling of '*Céilidh* Bar' on the facia, found the place all right.

It was cold for that bog, and it was nice and warm and jovially scholarly inside, with meat and drink of the best.

But I was between the devil and the deep sea—a Liberty boy and a Kerryman.

'When you're sure you're finished with the *Tishel Genewnack*[1] there, we'll have a run up to the sheep.'

So off he went. The bog itself was lovely in warm blues and browns that stretched as far as the horizon, and the sky bright with a Christmas glitter.

The sheep, when we got near enough to them, were munching away, not minding anyone, and I felt kind of sorry for them going off to be assassinated. But I consoled myself by thinking that they weren't going to be croaked just yet. They would all live to see their progeny next spring.

I thought of Tolstoy's remark in *War and Peace* to the effect that when a sheep is taken from the common fold to be specially fattened, the other sheep, watching his more rapid growth in the neighbouring and specially favoured pasture, must consider him almost in the light of a god, so much fatter

[1] Gaelic for 'Possessive Case'.

than themselves does he become. And when he leaves for the slaughter-house, and they see him no more, they must come to the conclusion that he has been divinely translated to fresh fields and pastures new, by supernatural intervention.

By the time I had chased after a few of them I'd more than Tolstoy to worry me.

It is said that the commander of a Japanese submarine that came to Cork was asked what he thought of it, and he replied that the only difficulty he and the crew had was in distinguishing one Corkman from another.

I had thought the same of sheep. But it wasn't long after I had dug myself out of the muck of the County Kildare for the first time, that I began to recognize one sheep from the next.

There was one vicious female criminal that persisted in

waiting until they were all nearly at wherever they were supposed to be going. Then she'd take a sly run round in the opposite direction, leading half the gang after her.

I'd know her, and I'd know the sixth generation of her, if I caught her looking up at me from a slab in Moore Street, ten years from now, if God leaves either one of us our health.

However, we got them off to Dublin and we went back into Billy's, where I heard the complaints of one man to another.

'You did. You called me out in the pouring rain to walk home with you, and then you got into the car and drove off.'

The muck drying on me and a tumbler in my hand, I settled down to listen to a bit of human argument and rest myself from sheep.

I meet a Sheik

*

I WAS IN THE STRAND recently—I should have said the Strand, London, in case people thought I meant the North Strand and I didn't get the credit of my travels.

Irish people, who for some reason have the reputation of being insular, have great *meas*[1] for the traveller.

It's almost a competition. A man from Ballyhaunis will, no doubt, get great credit for his weekly run to Sligo or Athlone. But he has to shut up about the glories of both places, when Micky Fitz that's working above in Dublin, comes down in the summer holidays.

And the Dubliner, on a visit to smaller centres in the west, or south, will almost certainly be introduced to some mild old man who stands innocently at the counter, and plies your man with questions about the wonders of the great metropolis, listening with wide-eyed astonishment to descriptions of traffic-lights and buses, and the flashing jewels of neon signs that shine across the width of O'Connell Street to one another.

The old man greets the account of metropolitan majesty, from Store Street Station to O'Keefe's the knacker's, with 'Oh' and 'Ah' and 'Glory be' and your gills is condescendingly pleased to have brought a hint at least, of the colour and busting life of urban civilization into the old man's last days, until he discovers that the old pig-minder has been getting it up for him, rich and rare. That he spent forty year in a saloon on Broadway, or drove a truck for Al Capone in Chicago, and

[1] Respect.

55

that he performs this Simple Simon act on every visiting Dubliner for the benefit of his friends and neighbours, who are in no way averse to seeing the jackeen being made look a gilly.

For some reason, the old fellow who has been to America is better thought of than the fellow who only got as far as Liverpool. I think they must sit up with maps measuring the distance, so as to know to what honours the returning exile is entitled.

In hotels and bars, in Youghal, Caherciveen, Donaghadee, Tallaght, Camden Town, Inisheer, and Kilburn—in any place where our people have gathered—I have bested them all.

If someone said he had been to Texas, and hunted cattle, I was hot on his heels with my story of a week-end spent with a sheik in East Tunis.

By the same token I met the sheik under rather peculiar circumstances. He fancied himself as something of a huntsman, but there was very little to be hunted in his own country, unless you count the sand-flies.

So when he was invited by the French Government to shoot deer in the Vosges he was delighted, and would hardly go to bed the night before the hunt was to begin.

But in the field he proved a very bad shot. The only deer he would have got a direct hit on would have been the one in the hall, and they wanted that for a hat-rack.

The French were very anxious to keep on the right side of the old sheik, and they didn't know what to do, till the next morning he sneaked out on his own, and they heard the bang and the crash of his guns, and squeals of delight in Arabic, not to mention the thud of falling bodies as his victims hit the dust.

He ran in ecstatically, and screeching in his own language: 'All of them have I killed, the woolly white deer.'

And when they followed him out they discovered about twenty tons of dead prime mutton belonging to the neighbouring farmer.

He was duly fixed up with a sum of money that more than compensated him for the loss of his 'woolly white deer', and

the old sheik returned home with a shipload of stuffed sheep's heads, which trophies of the chase now line the walls of his castle in Beni Rah Kosi.

How did I come into the story? I tied the fifty-six-pound weights on the legs of the sheep the previous night, with the man who owned them, a chap from Granamore, County Wicklow, by the name of Mike Burke.

I nearly drove a man in this city mad with yarns the like of that the other night.

He was standing at the counter with his friends, and smiled when he heard my accent. His own was an Irish one heavily mixed with Paddington. He paid tribute to the country of his adoption with the vowels, but the 'th's' betrayed the land of his birth.

' 'Ello, you're from Ahland. Just come oveh, Paddy?'

'That's right. Guilty on both counts.'

He smiled indulgently. 'Ah bin ere nah abaht fifteen years. Dow now when Ah was 'ome last.'

'I got in today from Baghdad.'

'From wheah?'

'Baghdad. I'm over here for an operation.'

'From Baghdad? For an operation? For what?'

'Leprosy. I'll tell how I got it. There was this sheik I knew. Man be the name of Mohammed Ali Bababa. Lived in a place be the name of Beni Rah Kosi. . . .'

He was once Crippen,
the piper

*

'IN THE BRITISH MILISHA he was, my poor fellow, wasn't he, Maria Concepta? And a fine man, too,' said Mrs. Brennan.

'He was all that,' said Maria Concepta, 'and I heard my own fellow saying that your fellow was as safe as houses in the war. He only had to put on his busby and march away. The Boers thought it was a hedgehog moving.'

'But all the same, I was thrilled to bits waiting for him to finish his month's training on the Curragh. I was faithful to him the whole four weeks and when the dread millingterry word of command rang out, and the period of separashing was over, and the sergeant-major roars, "Milisha to your work-houses, poor-houses, doss-houses and jails, disperse!" there I was, standing behind him, waiting to pick him up as he fell out. To pick him up and carry him home.'

'Aye, indeed,' said Maria Concepta. 'A tough little man he was, too, like the day he punched the countryman in the ankle for asking him whether he was a child or a midget.'

'Were you ever in the Army, Mister Cripping, sir?'

Crippen gave a mirthless laugh.

'Was I ever what? Are you codding me or what? Are you getting it up for me or what? Was I ever in the Army? Did you ever hear of the Malpas Street ambush? Did you ever hear of the attack on O'Keefe's the knacker's? Did you ever hear of the assault on the Soap Works in Brunswick Street? Or the raid on the Sloblands? Did yous?' He glared at me. 'Well, God almighty, that's the Irish all over. Did *you* ever hear tell

of the dead who died for Ireland? Well, you're looking at one
of them.'

'I'm sorry for your trouble,' I muttered, for want of something to say.

'I suppose yous never heard of the pitched battle at the Back
of the Pipes? And I suppose, talking about pipes, yous never
heard of the lone piper who played at the massacre of
Mullinahack? There was a song written about it.

'I was not long learning the pipes. But now yous know it, I
don't mind telling yous that my nickname in the old Seventh
Batt. was the Cock of the North.

'That was really on account of me mother keeping the
poultry above in Phibsboro. Ah, when I think of the old
days . . .' He sighed, looking into the depths of his tumbler.

'I was through the whole lot. The Tan War, the Civil War,
the Economic War.'

'Ah, more luck to you,' said Maria Concepta. 'Didn't I sing
for the boys?'

'You sang?' I asked.

'She did, Brending Behing. If you heard her singing *Home to
Our Mountings* you'd know all about it,' said Mrs. Brennan.

'I don't doubt you,' said I.

'That woman,' said Crippen, pointing to Maria Concepta,
'was principal soprano in the Hammond Lane.'[1]

'That's right,' said Mrs. Brennan, 'in the Hammongd Laying
Fouingdry Choir.'

'I suppose,' said I, with a weak grin, 'yous put on that opera
The Rose of Castile. Have you me? *The Rows of Cast Steel*. It's
a joke,' I pleaded, 'from a book by a man by the name of
James Joyce.'

'Do you think,' said Crippen severely, 'we're all thicks and
idiots here? Certainly we heard of James Joyce, the man who
wrote *Useless*. I was in the inntellimigentzia . . .'

I'd forgotten Crippen's connection with the world of letters.
He had knowledge of a bookie who took stamped addressed

[1] A Dublin foundry.

envelopes and International Reply Coupons to the odds and
ran to this bookie regular errands for both members of the
staff of a cultured quarterly, since deceased.

'Be the way, what happed your gills?'

'The former assistant editor?'

'Of course. D'you think I was enquiring about the char-
woman?'

'He's still with the B.B.C.'

'I wonder, Mr. Cripping, if you'd ever give me youngest
grandchild's eldest a bit of a note to him? He's the next one of
me descedings to leave school and at the moment he seems fit
for nothing but to be this year's net-ball champying. He's mad
to be an enjing-driver, and if your friend in the C.I.E.
could——'

'It's not the C.I.E.,' said Crippen, 'it's the B.B.C.'

'I beg your parding, Mr. Cripping.'

'Give us that bit offa song you sang in the Trouble,' said
Crippen in the direction of Maria Concepta.

'I might as well. Wait till I clear me throat.'

A sound as of the death-rattle came from under her shawl and

then, without further warning, a most blood-curdling moan went through the shop, as she threw back her covering and bayed the ceiling. 'Howl, howl, *howl . . .*'

The cat glanced anxiously round and at the third note got down from the window and ran out the door.

'You never lost it,' said Crippen, nodding his head in appreciation.

Maria Concepta screwed up her face another bit, and went on 'Howl! How long will dear old Ireland be unfree?'

'Lovely,' muttered Mrs. Brennan, rapping on the counter, and humming to herself. ' "Oh, never marry a soldier, an airman or a maree-ing, if you can get a rebel in his uniform of gree-ing . . ." '

The Hot Malt Man
and the Bores

*

' "WIPE YOUR BAYONET, Kinsella, you killed enough." '

'Go on,' says I.

'That's genuine,' said Kinsella, 'that's what Lord Roberts says to me in Blamevontame in 'nought one. I knew him before, of course, from the time we were in Egg Wiped. "Shifty Cush!" says Bobs, when he seen me on parade, "is that you, Kinsella?" "It is," says I, coming smartly to attention. "Who were you expecting?"

' "You've killed enough of bores," says Bobs.'

There was a sharp-featured gentleman sitting beside us having a drop of malt, hot. A great odour of cloves and old Irish rose from him as he turned round. He glared at Kinsella in a nationalistic fashion. 'That did you great credit, I'm sure. The bores never done this little country any harm for you to be killing them. Are you an Irishman?'

'I am,' says Kinsella. 'Are you a bore?'

'*Ná bac leis* whether I am or not,' says Hot Malt. 'The bores was always good friends of this little country, and I don't see what call you had to go killing them.'

The Bottle of Stout man glanced nervously up from his bus guide and spoke querulously at us. 'Sure what's the good of arguing over that now? Wouldn't they all be dead of old age be this time, anyway?'

'I don't see why they should be,' said Hot Malt. 'This mercenary foe of theirs is alive yet.'

'Look at here,' says Kinsella, 'I'm no Mendecency foe of

anyone. Maybe you know more about the Mendecency Institution than anyone else in this lounging bar.'

The Bottle of Stout man glanced again at his bus guide and called the assistant. 'How much is your clock fast?'

'The usual ten minutes, Mister O'.'

'I see, I see; bring us another bottle.' Then he fell to anxious calculations. 'It'd leave the Parkgate at eight-forty and to the Pillar at eight-forty-eight, say, and . . .' He glanced round again and we saw the front of a bus come past the window. The Bottle of Stout man fell to the floor like a trained guerilla fighter and cowered below the level of the window.

The bus drew alongside the stop outside the pub and its top floor was on a dead level with the lounge in which we sat. The narrowness of the street made ourselves and the passengers intimate spectators of each other.

Only one of them took advantage of the proximity thus afforded: a hatched-faced oul' strap who swept the features of each of us with a searching sharpness and then, not altogether satisfied with what she'd seen, nodded grimly and almost threateningly as the bus bore her off.

'Eh,' says Kinsella, 'that was a dangerous-looking oul' one that looked in at us off the bus—the one with the face of a D.M.P.[1] man.'

The Bottle of Stout man rose to his feet, and after a look out the window, turned to Kinsella, who nodded and said, 'You didn't miss much there, she's a right hatchet, whoever she is.'

'Excuse yourself,' said the Bottle of Stout man, 'she is my wife, and I'll thank you to keep a civil tongue in your head.' He spoke round at the company. 'You can't expect a man to put up with remarks like that about the woman he loves.'

Heads were nodded approvingly, and Kinsella was in some confusion.

'How was I to know she was your wife? And how did you know yourself it was her I was talking about? You were sitting on the floor and didn't see her.'

'I recognized her from your description,' said the Bottle of Stout man, with the quiet dignity of a trained mind.

An elderly lady in the corner shook her head and murmured enigmatically into her port: 'As the ole oopera says, "What the eye doesn't see the heart won't grieve for." I love you because you love her. Love's young dream, as I always said about my poor spowce: "Better the divil you know than the one you don't." '

'But anyway,' says Kinsella, resuming his conversation with me, 'the first man I sees at zero hour one-two—this was in the next war—was Jowls Loughrey, of the Dirty Shirts.

' "Halt," says he, "who goes there?"

' "It's me, Jowls," says I. "Whacker Kinsella from Messer Street—down beside the hospital."

---

[1] Dublin Metropolitan Police (before 1921).

' "Don't be so familiar with your 'Jowls'," says Jowls. "How do I know you're not German?"

' "I can't speak a word of German," says I. "I'm from Messer Street."

' "That doesn't prove anything," says Jowls, "I'm from Francis Street and I can't speak a word of French—how some ever I'll take your word for it. The attack is off. We can't go over the top kicking the football in front of us tonight."

' "Why not?" says I. "The men in my spittoon was looking forward to the bit of exercise."

' "They're after losing the ball," says Jowls.'

Just at that moment the Bottle of Stout man, after a hurried look at his bus guide and at the clock, fell to the ground, swift as before.

'Like one of them syrup-pots,' said Kinsella admiringly.

But he was not swift enough.

The lady shouted in from the top of the bus.

'I saw you,' she screeched, 'dodging down there, hiding on the floor. Making a jeer of your poor wife with your drunken bowseys of companions.' We all visibly blenched and cowered down, not on the floor altogether with the Bottle of Stout man, but with our faces not far off it. 'I know yous, you low lot. Tell him to get up off the floor now the bus is moving.'

It moved and we rose again.

'Don't mind me asking you,' asked the Hot Malt of the Bottle of Stout man. 'Why is it you don't go in another pub where she can't see you?'

The Bottle of Stout man sighed. 'You must forgive a sentimental old fool.'

'Certainly, certainly so,' muttered Kinsella, 'as an old soldier, I concur.'

The Bottle of Stout man wiped his eyes. 'This is how we met. She looked in at me off the top of a tram. I'll never forget it.'

Said the Hot Malt, 'Neither will we.'

Nuts from the Crimean War

*

ROUND OUR WAY there were many candidates for the brain garage. They were victims of the Great War, as it used to be called; the Black and Tan War, the Civil War, and the Economic War, when we were all a bit hatcha from eating free beef.

Mrs. Leadbeater could have been nuts from the Crimean War—she was old enough—but like many another she was mad in her own right.

Her sister, Mrs. Moneypenny, never recovered from a trip she'd made to Howth in the late summer of 1912, when she came back believing she had been turned into a lobster, and was ever after apprehensive of the death she would suffer if the people decided to eat her.

The sight of a pot of water, hot or cold, was enough to send her screeching from the kitchen. When she was finally brought back she would appeal to all and sundry not to put her in the pot.

Her first appeals were on the grounds of compassion, but she varied it by pointing out to the people that they wouldn't get much off her, anyway.

In Summerhill there was a German fishmonger called Frankenstein for short, and he used to run in the back of the shop when he saw her coming and leave the messenger boy to face her.

Sorrowfully she'd look down at the bright red bodies and claws on the slab, getting her emotions under control to give her screech in at the fugitive fishmonger: 'Murderer! Torturer! Who murdered my poor brothers and sisters!' And with a look in the direction of the dressed crab, 'and cousins!'

Then there was Mr. Aloysius Giltrap, who used to clap in the chapel and provoked Sergeant Cloonoe, who used to get his wife out on the floor at half-two in the morning doing foot-drill and bayonet practice with the sweeping-brush. But

personally, I always thought that the Corcorans of the back kitchen, Number Ten, beat them all over the distance.

Mrs. Corcoran was an old lady of some seventy summers, which, counting the winters, would leave her at the time of which I speak about a hundred and forty, which is what she looked and not a day more.

Her son Paddins was a sort of Neo-Old I.R.A. man and dressed for the part. He wore a cap, a sports coat with leather buttons and split up the middle and knee breeches. He resembled very much a picture of a fearsome character depicted on the *Cumann na nGaedheal* election posters of the time, which read: 'Vote for Us and Keep the Shadow of the Gunman from your Home.'

Very little chisellers like myself thought it was Paddins Corcoran on the poster and gave him great respect, but the big fellows used to greet him on the corner with salutes and standing to attention, and making him reports from the First Brigade, the Second Brigade, the Boys' Brigade and the Fire Brigade.

Poor Paddins would take it all for in the real, whereas it was only in the cod, and on Bodenstown Sunday[1] he was a sight to free Ireland. With only a look at him, the British would have given back the Six Counties and thrown the Isle of Man in for good measure.

He wore his cap, but turned back to the front with the peak down the back of his neck to show that he was ready for active service, and a pair of leggings he'd borrowed off L. S. D. Regan, the dairyman from Santry, also known on a less national scale as Long Skinny Dominic, whence the initials.

He also had a bandolier, grimly bulging with rolled pieces of paper and a water-bottle, over the sports coat.

At one of the street battles in Cathal Brugha Street that helped to pass the depression for the people, Paddins shouted up to a well-known public figure who was trying to address a meeting, 'You have the best of men in your jails, and I dare you to take me now.'

I may not, nor no one belonging to me, have agreed with his opinions, but the aforesaid figure was a Dubliner and seldom short of an answer. He leaned down from the platform to answer Paddins. 'I am not,' he said, 'a collector of curios.'

But with a fine disregard for the late Civil War, the chaps

[1] Theobald Wolfe Tone, fountainhead of Irish Republicanism, was buried in Bodenstown churchyard in 1798. There is an annual pilgrimage to his grave.

on the corner didn't mind getting it up for Joshua Carroll, who was a part-time soldier in the Government Army.

Joshua was called up for training a number of times a year and had to go away to a camp. During the winter he stood in the evening-time on the corner dressed in his green uniform, which for some reason had blue epaulettes. The big fellows had us chisellers trained to sing at him:

> 'If you're fed up with life,
> And you don't want a wife,
> Do what Joshua did,
> Join the Militia . . .'

Myself and my brothers joined in this, with function and capernosity, as true little Republicans, apart from the excitement of annoying someone that was doing us no particular harm—an occupation indulged in, with less excuse, by many of us in later life—and were somewhat taken aback when Paddins Corcoran chased us and went to give our Rory a clout.

We expressed our indignation at such treachery, but Paddins said, 'I respect Joshua, as one soldier to another,' returned to the corner and saluted Joshua, who returned the salute, when both forces 'reconoythered' the position to see if they could make up between them the price of two pints.

Meet a great poet

*

'BRENDING BEHING.'

 'Good morning, Mrs. Brennan.'

 'And good luck.'

 'As the crow said to the duck.'

 'You too, Maria, and your friends in America.'

 'What I want to know is, where might you be going with the Rennington? Not a visit to your uncle, so early in the morning?'

 'There's much value in scrap these days,' muttered Crippen, from a corner. He has literary ambitions himself and bitterly resents any pretensions in that direction on the part of anyone else. The sight of my battered old typewriter is a cause of severe illness to him. If I wanted to see him jump off Butt Bridge, I'd only have to walk down East Arran Street carrying a brief-case.

 'Ah, I don't know now,' said Maria, with an amiable sniff.

 'I know you don't,' said Crippen. 'I heard all about you. When the white gas meters came out, you were an hour trying to get into the *Balladmakers' Saturday Night*[1] on your one.'

 'Ah now, Mr. Cripping. Maria's not all that bad. She can count her change lovely if whatever it is she's buying hasn't gone up from the last time she bought it. We can't all be cheenises like yourself and Brending Behing there.'

 'And if you want to know,' said I, 'I'm taking this machine to be cleaned and oiled.'

[1] A Radio Eireann programme of ballad-singing.

'And it's not all that bad of a machine, Mr. Cripping. Do you not remember the testimoleum he did for poor Henrietta on it?'

'I do not,' said Crippen.

'Ah, don't you remember? He came here one morning and poor Henrietta, she used to follow painters, cleaning houses and washing up their dirt after them, before she took to the lifting, and then she wasn't able to get a job on account of not having a testimoleum, and where would she get it, barring they'd give her one out of the "Joy",[1] but Brending Behing here sat down in the corner, opened up the yoke and there and then wrote her a beauty of a reverence.

'You'd have got yourself a job on the strent of it. To the effect that she was the nanny of his children till they were big enough to beat her, and he knew that she was a life-long teetotaller and a lovely knitter, with a soft hand under a duck,

[1] Mountjoy Prison.

72

and to who it might concern and them it didn't, could go and do the other, and it had his signature and all to it. What was it now? Lord Williamstown and Booterstown and Monkstown and . . .'

'Blanchardstown,' suggested Maria, helpfully.

'And she got a lovely position with some old one from England and took everything that wasn't nailed down, only they caught her carrying out the sundial. Very unlucky thing to be caught with.'

'I know this much,' said Crippen, 'if I was doing me writing, I couldn't do it on one of them things.'

'God knows and you're right there, Mr. Crippen. I'd like to see the bookies, the day of a big race, and everyone trying to write their three cross-doubles and the same back, on them things. All them machines going together you'd think it was the Hammond Lane[1] you were in, and how would a body hear a result or anything?'

'I wasn't talking about writing three cross-doubles,' said Crippen, crossly.

'Well, accumalators, wouldn't they be worse, and——'

'I was talking about writing poetry,' said Crippen, in some exasperation. I mean, looking as if bad words would be sullying his lips any minute.

'Oh, yes, Mr. Cripping. Now I have you.'

He looked sternly at me. 'Tell me any great poem that was written on one of them things?'

'Well,' said I, 'I was going to say that I didn't stand over the shoulders of great poets to know what way they went about it.'

'Well, well,' quoted Crippen, 'that's what you look for when the beer runs out. But you can't answer me. And remember I wrote poems before you come up. *And* translations from the English language, the Irish language . . .'

'The deaf and dumb language,' offered Maria.

---

[1] A Dublin foundry.

'I didn't know you wrote Irish,' said I.

'You didn't know. You didn't know because you never went to the trouble of finding out.'

'Well, say one now, Mr. Cripping; go on, say it up now and the divil thank the begrudgers.'

'I'll say it, though seeing as yous don't understand the language yous won't be much the better of it.'

He looked round at the audience and fixed Maria with an arrogant glance. 'Like a sow looking into a swill barrel,' he muttered elegantly.

'I know a bit of Irish,' said I.

'You do, but it's only the new stuff they have in the schools. Dots and dashes. But this is the real goat's toe.'

He cleared his throat and began:

> 'Pillaloo, wirrastroo,
> Sure I'm kilt,
> May the quilt
> Rest lightly on your beautiful form,
> When the weather is hot, or

(he waved a complacent hand)

> 'Again when it's not,
> I'll roll you up,
> Cosy and warm.'

'That's massive,' said Mrs. Brennan. 'Have you e'er another one? I could folly nearly every word of that.'

'This one is a lot harder.'

'Well, never mind, it's all for the cause. Me poor father had a lovely pone called, *Never Hit a Lady With Your Hat On*, but it was only English.'

'Hhhhm,' said Crippen, clearing his throat and throwing out his hand in declamation:

'Come out, my shillelagh,
Come out, love, to me,
On the bright Cruiskeen Lawn
We will dance the Banshee;
And while bright shines the moon,
Lady Luna above,
In the groves of Na Bocklesh
We'll lovingly rove.
And softly and sweetly I'll murmur to you,
Musha and allanna, astore, tiggin too.'

'Massive,' muttered Mrs. Brennan, rubbing her eye. 'Oh, leave it to you, Mr. Cripping!'

But going out, Michael called me and said out of the side of his mouth, 'He never made them poems up.'

'No?'

' 'Course he didn't. They were written by Yeets. Y'often heard of him; owned the Half-Way House above in Drimnagh.'

Here's how history is written

*

'HE HAD A FACE like a plateful of mortal sins,' said the Bard.

'G'way,' said Crippen, 'you haven't a snap?'

'There wasn't much snaps going that time,' said the Bard, 'and our Provoke Sergeant, it was trying to forget him we were after we got away from him, not to be carrying round snaps or pictorial representations of him one way or another, except if he was swinging the wrong end of a rope. But that was the British Army for you, them times.'

'Well,' sighed Crippen, resignedly, 'to hear of a fellow the like of that, it'd kind of resign you to what me and me likes did to the same British Army afterwards. Aye, even if I done jail over it.'

'More luck to you,' muttered an old fellow, grimly, from the corner.

'Arrested, I was, at the Curragh races of 'twenty-one and charged with obtaining money by means of a trick—to wit, Find the Lady and The Sliced Woman—from a few Tommies that was only after coming over for training.

'I took twenty-two bar off them, but pleaded in the court that we were entitled to some of our own back after all England robbed on us, and me solicitor said it was only plaguing the Egyptians, but the old beak said they weren't the Egyptians but the West Kents, and I got weighed off with six months. But I wasn't the only decent man in jail that time.'

'Bedad, you weren't,' said the old man, with a twisting of

76

his gums. 'Aye, and many's the decent man was hung, and not a word about him.'

I struck up, to the air of the *Rising of the Moon*, and with vehemence:

> 'They told me, Francis Hinsley,
> They told me you were hung . . .'

'Good on you,' said the old man, his hand on his ear, for fear he'd miss one word.

> 'With red protruding eyeballs . . .'

'More luck to me one son,' said the old man, in tears of content.

> ' . . . and black protruding tongue.'

'Ah, your blood's worth bottling,' screeched the old man.

'Is that one of Yeets's?' asked Crippen.

'No, that was written by Evelyn Waugh,' said I.

'And bedad and she wasn't a bad one, either,' said Crippen, shaking his head. ' "I'll dress myself in man's attire and fight for liberty," what? Eveleen was far from being the worst. What was this crowd she was with, now? I just can't think of it for the minute.'

'Wasn't it the Belcuddy Battalion, or the First Battalion of the Third Belcuddy Brigade?' said I. 'You should know that, Crip, above anyone.'

He spat on the floor and looked seriously round the company. 'Not a man in Ireland should know better.'

'What part of the country would that be now?' asked the Bard, who is himself a native of the far north, Ballymoney direction.

'What part of the country?' asked Crippen, incredulously. 'Is it coddin me y'are, or what?'

He looked over at the old man.

'Can you believe your ears? A man here does not know where,' he paused a minute, 'er . . . eh . . .'

'Belcuddy,' said I.

'That's right,' said Crippen. 'Belcuddy is.'

The old man looked over and waved his stick: '*Ná bac leis.*[1] Leave him to God!'

Crippen fixed the Bard with a severe look.

'Certainly. I'd a thought anyone would a known that. Nawbocklesh. It's about eight mile this side of it. Nice little town, too.' His lips softened in a reminiscent smile. 'Nawbocklesh,' says he, 'and the blue sky over it.'

Crippen sighed, and the old man gazed on the floor, thinking of old times, and ground his gums together with a noise like a sand lorry on the mountain road outside.

I raised my eyes to the ceiling and opened my mouth in a patriotic fashion:

[1] 'Don't mind him.'

'Oh, down in Belcuddy they fought the glorious fight,
All through the day and through most of the night,
And never knocked off, for sup, bit or bite . . .'

'Ah, me good-living youth,' said the old man.

'Ah, there was great men in the country that time,' said Crippen.

'Aye, and women, too, like the one that wrote the bit of a song your gills there was singing.'

'Is it Eveleen Warr?' asked my gills.

'The very woman. The Bardess of Belcuddy, we called her.' He looked at the Bard. 'You and her might have made a match of it. Set up in the bard line together. But I believe she was sweet on the Commandant and when he got killed in the Butter Tasting and Poultry Station, she never did an hour's good. It's all in a poem she wrote, the time of the death:

'I leave up me Thompson, and me short Webley,
Distribute me hand grenades among the foe,
I'm fed up fighting for dear old Ireland,
And to a convent I now will go.'

'A lovely thing that.'

Pity the poor man

*

BESIDES THE BARD, Crippen, myself and Mrs. Brennan, there was a duffel-coat in the corner containing, newly arrived off the Liverpool boat, a young Irish poet of uncertain age.

'No,' said Crippen, in answer to Mrs. Brennan, 'he's not a monk. That's a poet's get-up he has on. And he leans his head on his hands because it saves his energy for writing poems and roaring at the people. I'll just see if he's in form yet.'

'Ask him if he knoos that one o' Burns, *Hoo Crool*,' said the Bard.

Crippen went towards the recumbent form of the Y.I.P. and shook it. He looked round at the people and said, 'This is like a poem of Burns' and all, *The Wind that Shakes the Duffel-Coat.*'

'God forgive you, Mr. Cripping,' said Mrs. Brennan, 'you're a deeming.'

'Eh,' said Crippen in the ear of the Y.I.P., 'do you know that one of Burns' . . .'

The duffel-coat shook itself and the Young Irish Poet shook himself and glared at us with the fury of a newly woken squirrel.

'Do I know?' he screamed. 'Do I know? Woe! An ignorant, meritless crew are you——'

'I told you, Bard,' said Crippen, 'he'd leave you in the ha'-penny place. Words at will he has, rhymed and ready.'

'——crew are you. That never as much as glanced at the last

80

issue of *The Blunt Instrument,* the last of the little reviews with
the fifth of my cantos in it:

> 'Woe, there is a lot of it, flying round,
> More often the sound, sniff, sniff,
> Of woe,
> Than any of your damned ha, ha, ha, or
> Hoe, hoe, hoe.'

He slumped back in his duffel-coat and waved the back of
his hand to us before submerging again.

'Massive,' said Mrs. Brennan; 'especially the cursing at the
end.'

'Fine fellow,' said Crippen, 'You want to read a poem he
wrote one time called *Where Am I?* Took a degree in knowledge
at the National University, Trinity College, Dublin! Never did
a day's work in his life, but a lovely dancer.'

'Burns was the very same,' said the Bard.

'Oh, the very same,' said Crippen. 'You know, the bit where
he says:

> 'You may hay the growsy or the grunk,
> But a mon's a mon, a mon, a mon, a mon,
> An hay ye don't like it, I no care,
> To me, it's all the one.'

'I don't recall that bit,' said the Bard.

'And hard for you,' said Crippen, 'for it was never let out to
the ordinary public. 'Case the other crowd would be made as
wise as themselves. But I got it from the right quarter; chap in
the gas company. That's all fine and large, but I'm telling you
that it's not what you know but who you know; and a shut
mouth will catch no flies; better to be mean than at a loss, have
you me?'

'There's a lot in what you say,' said the Bard. 'I mind the
time I was in Dumfries. When I was in the Army.'

'Was in a Scotch regiment myself,' said Crippen, 'the Submarine Kilties. Deserted the time of the Economic War.

Wouldn't sell my own ould country. Besides, they started giving us New Zealand mutton.'

'Well, this was in the First War. I was after coming over from Larne, through Portpatrick, and enlisted in a moment of foolishness in the Scotch Terriers. They were a guid enough mob—they called them the "Dogs of War"—but the Provoke Sergeant——'

'The one with the face like a plateful of mortal sins?' asked Crippen.

'The very same,' said the Bard.

'Well,' said Crippen, 'just so as we'd know him.'

'I was left minding the canteen one night, an' what happened but I left a tap running when I'd fallen asleep. And there was nearly a hogshead short and the Provoke Sergeant wakes me up and says I was under close arrest and I could take me choice of being tried under military law and being shot for deserting my post by falling asleep under the barrel, or being tried under civil law and hung for sacrilege.

'To give me time to consider me position I was locked up in the guardroom, which was a wee place with a window looking down into the barrack yard thirty feet below.

'I looked around me and there was nothing in the guard-room but a water-jug, table and stool and a cupboard in the wall. There was nothing in the cupboard when I looked but a lot of rifle pull-throughs, lengths of cloth, three feet long. And I had an idea of a sudden.

'There was eleven of them. That meant thirty feet and something over for the knots. I could make a rope. No sooner said than done.

'I made me rope, attached one end to the window, slid down and over the wall and was on the road to Carlisle before you could say——'

'Mull o' Galloway,' said Crippen.

'But when I got to the border between Annan in Scotland and Longtown in England, what do I see but a sentry-box blocking me way to Carlisle and the London road and me with no papers. But I sneaks up beside the box and rubs me feet on the road, and the sentry shouts out, "Halt, who goes there?"

'I said it was me, and he shouts at me like he's talking to a half-fool:

' "And where do you think you're going this hour of the night?"

' "If you please sir, I want to get into Scotland. I live in Annan, and me mother will be worried about me."

' "You should have thought of that before twelve o'clock. Get back there, to the English side now, for your mother will have to do without you until morning. Come on now," he says, waving the rifle at me. "Get back there, and if I catch you trying to sneak into Scotland past this post, I'll put one through you, you loon, you."

'And he puts me on down the road and I'm safe and sound on the way to Carlisle.

'Till I got very tired after all the walking and sat down on an empty box on wheels, a sort of a watch-box, to rest myself,

and was only woken up by a low and savage growling, like a beast of prey.'

'The Provoke Sergeant?' said Crippen.

'No,' said the Bard, 'but what was nearly as bad. A ferocious-looking watch-dog.'

'An Allegation,' said Mrs. Brennan.

'There was only one thing to be done. Grab a hold of his tail. I manœuvred round as best I could till at last I got a grip on it, and he let a roar and a howl out of him like the Zoo on strike, but I held on till he tried to run away from me, and the watch-box went along on its wheels on the road, and the harder he pulled to get away from me, the tighter I gripped, till he drew me on the watch-box the whole way to Carlisle.

'Then, just as dawn rose over the spires of the town, I let go of the dog and he dropped down dead.'

Up and down Spion Kop

★

When I was young, I used to be,
As fine a man as e'er you'd see,
And the Prince of Wales, he says to me,
'Come, join the British Army.'

Toora loora loora loo,
They're looking for monkeys in the Zoo.
And if I had a face like you,
I'd join the British Army.

Sarah Curley baked the cake;
'Twas all for poor Kate Condon's sake,
I threw meself into the lake,
Pretending I was barmy.

Toora loora loora loo,
'Twas the only thing that I could do,
To work me ticket home to you,
And leave the British Army.

ON WEDNESDAYS and I a child, there were great gatherings
of British Army pensioners and pensionesses up on the corner
of the North Circular, in Jimmy-the-Sports'.

When the singing got well under way, there'd be old fellows
climbing up and down Spion Kop till further orders and other
men getting fished out of the Battle of Jutland, and while one
old fellow would be telling of how the Munsters kicked the
football across the German lines at the Battle of the Somme,

there'd be a keening of chorused mourners crying from under
their black shawls over poor Jemser or poor Mickser that was
lost at the Dardanelles.

Jimmy-the-Sports' Bar did not at all relish the British Army or
anything to do with it, but a publican is of a kind above politics.

My family would be shocked out of their boots at any of us
listening to such 'loyalist' carrying-on, but I—oh, woe to me
in the times of Republican wrath—I lusted after false gods,
and snaked in among the widows and orphans, and sat at the
feet of the veterans, to sell my country for a glass of Indian ale
and a packet of biscuits, and as Jembo Joyce would say, 'putting
up me two hands to thank heaven that I had a country to sell'.

Indian ale is a thing like the Ballybough tram—gone out.
It was sold out of a barrel in pubs and grocers' shops as well,
because it was a T.T. drink.

Us children were ardent T.T.'s because we thought it had
something to do with Stanley Woods and the Isle of Man races,
and with Doctor Pat O'Callaghan, Colonel Fitzmaurice, R. N.
Tisdall, John Joe Sheehy, Larry Cervi and Bertie Donnelly.

This Indian ale was like porter in appearance and it might
happen at these pension days in Jimmy-the-Sports', that glasses
would get mixed up and you wouldn't know what you were
getting, sitting down there on the floor out of sight and snap-
ping biscuits from one another.

Besides, the older ladies believed in a sup of porter for
children of pre-Confirmation age and even said, 'Let them
have a taste of it now and they'll never bother with it when
they're grown up.'

Sometimes, *mo bhron*,[1] these theories have little or no scien-
tific basis.

When the Imperial bounty of a grateful monarch had gone
a good way in the process of liquidation, one lady was sure to
stand up and sing a song about her late husband, who was a
machine-gunner and met some quicker machine-gunner on the
cousin's side.

[1] My sorrow.

My father always called it that, and said the dead or wounded of the Great War were an example to people not to be getting mixed up in family quarrels. And the Guelphs, Saxe-Gothas, Windsors, or whatever they call themselves, he regarded as the most dangerous clan in the whole of the world.

Besides, I knew the lady, and she was kind to all children, her own and any other ones, and she had a good voice, which is a thing I admire in a citizen, being no mean performer on the gargle trap myself.

Then Chuckles would stand up to give a bar. Chuckles, as far as I know, had not taken part in the European disturbances of 1914–18, nor had he played anything more than the part of a social worker in the wars of 1919–23 round the North Circular Road.

In time of siege he fed the civilian population with hams and sides of beef, augmented by flour and canned foods which he collected from the shops around. He described his collecting as 'armed begging' and only once did he meet with anything like a refusal.

At a big branch of an English combine, the manager's wife came down to say that her husband was phoning up head office in Liverpool to see what he could spare, that it was clearly contrary to the laws of God and man that people should benefit by war to the extent of eating things like ham that they never tasted in peace.

'I hope,' said Chuckles, with a pious glance at his Colt forty-five, 'your husband is in a state of grace.'

'Oh,' said the manager's wife when she saw the skit, 'I didn't know you were a milling-terry man. That's different. Will you give a receipt sir, please, with your name and rank?'

'Right,' said Chuckles, calling up his supporters.

When they'd filled the handcart, he gave his official receipt signed 'Me, Chuckles, O/C Looters,' saluted and went off.

My father died in war

*

I'M NOW GOING TO GIVE my eyewitness account of my father's death in action at the Dardanelles.

As I was saying before, I was a great attender at the celebrations of British Army pensioners and pensionesses on Wednesdays on our corner of the North Circular Road.

So this day they are all talking about a film that's on in the old Royal.

It was called *Tell England* when it was made, but they thought it more tactful to call it *Gallipoli* when it was shown here.

'Iz a mazziv pit-chewer,' said the Granny Carmody in Grenville Street language. 'Yez zee all the poo-war japs and the' coming offa the Brizidge battle chips and been mone dow-in in the wawdher.'

'What Japs, Granny?' I whispered up at her. 'Who were they up for in the war?'

'All the japs, the japs in the Dubal-ins—in the View-shalleers. Poor Bogo Brennan, hees ozziver was shot offa hees horse. A vunny plaze to brin' a horse, but the old quality couldn't be sebarazed-ed from their beastises. The'd even try and brin' them to bed widhem. Bogo said he lived three days on jockalate. Some said eh waz az much az ever he got at home, but all the japs waz livin on jockalate, at the Dardanelles.'

Us chisellers on the floor discussed the matter and agreed that the Dardanelles would not be a bad place to be if you got chocolate all the time as a principal article of diet, but we

gathered from the conversation of the men that there were
people living there called The Terrible Turks, and what they
did with you, if they got their hands on you, was a matter to
be whispered.

Tell England alias *Gallipoli* was a silent picture, technically
speaking.

The picture got off to a good start, with the fellow in the
orchestral stalls knocking hell out of his drum during the
bombardment of the shore batteries.

The next thing we saw was what we were waiting for—the
soldiers charging down the gang-planks of the landing-craft.

From every part of the gods the screeches went up, 'Oh,
there's our Mickser.' Other old ones screeched: 'Oh, take me
out, I can't stick it. There's me husband in the water.'

Granny Carmody was not to be bested and let a roar out of
her that you'd hear in Gallipoli, 'Oh, me own sweet onion,
there he is, me poor first husband's brother.'

As the face that appeared close up that moment was that of

a bearded Indian, I was very much impressed by the Granny's relations.

'Oh, there's me da.' I let out a roar for the good reason that you might as well be out of the world as out of the fashion.

'Ah, God help the poor child,' some old one screamed from behind, 'he's gone in a wakeness.' I wasn't, until she put the idea in my head and then I did and moaned, 'Da, da, da.'

The old one behind called for a nurse who was in attendance and I was brought to the manager's office and given tea and cake, while I told how I'd seen my daddy killed by one of them Turks. To tell the truth, I thought the Turks was a family, and that Turk was their name like Behan was mine.

'Don't mind the dirty little liar. Hees father was in the I.R.Ah,' said the Granny Carmody. The next thing there was a loud crash from outside and windows smashed and plaster fell off the wall. 'That drum-player again,' said the Granny; 'he should be more careful.'

Tenor of the streets

*

'AT THE ZOOAHLOGICAL MOMENT you'll recover your perpiscasity,' said Crippen.

'Oh Mr. Cripping, sir, you have words at will, so you have,' said Mrs. Brennan. 'And one sure five—if you didn't go to school, you met the scholars on the way back.'

'Oh, he went further nor ha'penny book, ma'am, not but what,' said Maria Concepta, looking at me, 'there's no green in your eye, either, if it went to that.'

'Brending Behing is odious from educayshing, Maria, and could be a good newspaper chap if only he put himself to it. And he's a lovely voice to scream the readers. My father was gorgeous at it. He used to start off on a kind of low "doh".'

She raised her voice in the manner of a newsvendor and filled the shop with a howl that sent Michael's cat running hell for leather up Chancery Place.

'It be the ha-ha, dough-eeeeee.'

'Lovely, indeed,' said I.

'When my father would shout that—"Football results" it meant—you'd see the people looking round the length of O'Connell Street. He had a beautiful voice all right and the time Giggly was over singing in the Royal, they were thinking of taking him up.'

'Small blame to them,' muttered Crippen.

'And sending him to Rome.'

'Not far enough.'

'That's right, Mr. Cripping, sir, if you'd only have heard him. For to have his voice trained. And his last wish was for a

bit of music. We put on the record; even now, I can't bear to think of it.'

'I'd say so,' said Crippen. 'But, cheer up; we won't be that long after him. You were crying after your late spouser earlier this morning.'

'Ah, poor little Dimples, Maria. I was going through a few little odds and ends at home, when I came across the summings he got the time he was had up for lifting the conger eel out of the market above.

' "I only took it to practice with me tin whistle, and get an honest living snake-charming, the same as I have seen them doing in India with the Dublins, when I was out there in 'ninety-two," says he.

' "And did you have to put it in a pot with three half onnings to do that?" says the magistrate.

' "If you want to know," says I to him, "they weren't onnings but shallots."

' "Remove that persing," said he, but before they shifted me I was not long telling him that I was no persing, nor no one belonging to me. But it went to me heart when I saw that summings, thinking of poor Dimples.'

'And where do you leave me own poor fellow?' said Maria Concepta, with a slight sniff. 'Poor Pappan. He was born near Man-of-War in the year 'seventy-one. He could easy be here, this very morning.'

'So could Parnell,' said Crippen.

'A lovely man, too,' said Maria, 'like we used to sing in the old National Tantrum, "We'll have no chief but Charlie." But they're all gone now.'

'Two poor widow wimming is what we are,' said Mrs. Brennan. 'Michael, come up here.'

'Ah, yes,' said Crippen, appreciatively, 'the injection of consolation.'

'The injeckshing of consolayshing,' nodded Mrs. Brennan, adding, 'and two pints for the menkinds, Michael.'

'Sure, when relaxation sets in yous won't know yourself,' said Crippen. 'It's a wonder yous don't take a ramble down as far as Ringsend of a Saturday night.

'There's a pub there and it's all widows. Young widows, old widows, thin widows, fat widows, rich widows and poor widows. They sit there talking about their husbands all night, till nine o'clock, when they start crying over them.'

'You might call that pub a boo-hoozer,' said I.

'There's no call to be making game of the people,' said Crippen. 'Some of your lithery friends wouldn't last long down there. They don't like Bohemians in Raytown.'[1]

'I know,' said I, 'they'd sooner have Shelbourne.'

'I heard of that place you're talking about, Mr. Crippen,' said Maria Concepta. 'All the widow women, when they're done crying, sit round reading the deaths in the paper to see who'll be coming in the next Saturday night, and passing the paper from one to another.'

'That's right,' said I, 'they call it the boo-hoo's Who.'

'This,' said Crippen, 'must be your witty half-hour.'

---

[1] Bohemians: a Dublin football team somewhat despised in Ringsend (Raytown), where Shelbourne A.F.C. have their ground.

We took over a castle

*

YOU MAY find it hard to believe that I was ever an invited guest in a castle, but in my childhood I spent a great number of months in one as such.

This is how it happened. My connection with the agricultural interest and with the backbone of the country was so slight, that when the teacher was explaining how much we owed the farmers of Ireland and asked me where our food came from, I replied, 'Summerhill,' and when that strapping Christian Brother moved towards me in a manner that behoved no good to Brendan Francis Aidan Behan, though I knew I had given the wrong answer, the only alternative that came readily to mind was 'Dorset Street'.

I had no relations on a farm, and was not personally acquainted with a single farmer. I approved of farmers, particularly from Tipperary or West Cork, because I had heard older people speaking of Dan Breen and Tom Barry.

> They were shot in pairs
> Coming up the stairs
> By Sean Treacy and Dan Breen.

Both of whom knew how to handle the Black and Tans. Anyhow up to quite an advanced age I did not know they used real horses at the races. I thought it was all done with telephones.

But I had never heard of the Anglo-Irish. I knew there were

95

Protestants, because I played with half a dozen of them. I knew there were Jews, because I knew some and they had a cemetery in Fairview, and I thought they were a pretty daft lot because they had the date '5683' written on the stone over the door, though one of them from our way did write *Did Your Mother Come From Ireland*. But that was later than the time I was in the castle.

Well, who let me into the castle? It was this way. A relation of mine was a young chap in the cattle trade. He was as good a judge of a beast as you'd get from here to Mulhuddart, though he was born round the North Circular Road, the same as the rest of us, and learned all he knew up in Prussia Street, working for a salesmaster.

There was this castle out in the County Dublin, and the people that owned it left it for a bit, because they got nervous during the Civil War.

But the place, from being left empty, was being ruined from damp and going to rack and ruin and all to that effect, and the people who owned it wrote from Margate or Miami, or wherever they were, and asked the salesmaster would he get someone to go and live in it for a bit.

To cut the long story short, our Richie, the young cattle fellow, said he didn't mind and out he went.

The next thing was, of a Sunday, my Granny and two of her sisters went out on a visit to see how he was getting on, and my granny said the air was a very good thing out there and would do all the good in the world to her other poor sister, Henrietta.

Poor Henrietta caught a bad cold at Parnell's funeral and hadn't been expected to live this forty year. She was only able to lie in bed and moan, 'Is any of yous ever going to make the drain of tea?'

When the teacup was not actually at her lips, she was bemoaning the fact that she was a 'poo—er orpher-a-n'. I ran out of the *Phantom of the Opera* because Lon Chaney put me in mind of her.

It was decided that the bit of air would do me good too and I joined the merry house-party, but damned nearly passed out because they gave me a room to myself. I was eventually brought in with my granny, for I didn't think much of this solitary-confinement act.

Our team was playing in the final of the Conway Cup in the Fifteen Acres, and the boys decided this was good for collective training. So they came out too, bringing with them a gramophone and a record with two sides to it, *On Mother Kelly's Doorstep* and *Gee, oh Gosh, oh Golly, I'm in love with Molly*. And a fellow called 'Thirsty' that trained greyhounds.

My Aunt Henrietta sat in the window over a field at the back to watch the team practising, and would shout dog's abuse at the players if everything wasn't going to her liking. 'Thirsty' said they wouldn't mind him keeping the dogs in the drawing-room for a while. The kennels were leaking at home and it wasn't doing them any good.

Our Richie said the place was a cross between a sports' ground, a sanatorium and a relief scheme, and he was fit for the puzzle factory, and they said he could go on up there; they'd look after the castle till he came out.

We had a dance on a Sunday night. There were a lot of girls working in factories at that time, and they used to bring out cigarettes and sandwiches and cake for the team, and after tea there was dancing to the record, one side after the other, turn about being fair play.

Everything went like a canal boat up a hill till this Sunday night Richie came up, all white and pale, like someone on a week-end pass out of Glasnevin.[1]

'You must have got a bad result,' said 'Thirsty'.

'I'll be put up in the "Joy",'[2] moaned Richie.

'It was the Gorman[3] yesterday,' said our outside-left. 'But a change is as good as a rest and it'll be nearer your work.'

'They're coming up the drive. Right now.'

So they were; the people that owned the place.

'Quick,' said the outside-left, 'out in the grounds the lot of yous.'

'Someone of yous wait here and give me a hand with me aunt.'

She was asleep, for once in a way, and they dumped her in a closet and left her there. The others went out with the foot-ballers.

'I only hope them this-and-that dogs keeps easy,' muttered Richie to himself.

'I hope so and all,' said I.

'Oh, I'd forgotten you. What am I going to do with you?'

'I know,' said I. 'I can get under the dead dog in the front room.'

'That's not a dead dog, it's a dead tiger; but go on, get under it, only hurry.'

[1] Glasnevin Cemetery.
[2] Mountjoy Prison.
[3] Grangegorman: the Dublin Mental Home.

I did and only in time, for the next thing I heard the door open and this old one, and an old fellow, speaking to Richie.

They weren't gone very far when I heard a long and deep moaning.

'Cedric,' said the old one, very shiveringly, 'did you hear that? It's the banshee.'

But it wasn't. Only 'Thirsty's' old bitch. She moaned again.

'Don't you think we'd s-s-see it better by daylight, C-Cedric?'

Cedric said nothing, but the next thing my Aunt Henrietta woke in her closet and moaned out through the door: 'Is any a yous ever going to make the dr-a-in a te-a-a? Sure, I'm only a poo-er . . .'

But the old one let a screech out of her and ran for the door and down the gravel path, leading Cedric by a short head.

What did I do? Just lay under the tiger, that's all. My Aunt Henrietta would scare you, even if you were used to her. You should have heard her!

Remember Duck-the-Bullet

*

'PRESS,' said Mrs. Brennan. We looked at her with a note of interrogation on each countenance; my own, Crippen's, and Maria Concepta's. That is to say if you could describe the last-mentioned as a countenance.

'Press,' said Mrs. Brennan, 'and dresser and chester-drawers and wardrobe, he'd leave them all in smithereens, and small-sized ones at that, when the fit came on him. Poor ould Duck-the-Bullet. It was really a kind of homesickness made him do it. Homesickness for the Somme in 1916.

'But be the time he'd finished with the furniture you wouldn't know the difference between the North Lotts and Flanders. And the drilling was the worst. His poor wife Esther Judas, Ace we called her for short, though she preferred Judy herself, and the daughter Nono, that was named in honour of *No, No, Nanette*, that was on in the Roto next door to the hospital when she was born, would have to get up in the middle of the night and stand there, while he charged them up and down the room with the sweeping-brush and showed them how to point and parry.'

'Well, I always say,' said Maria Concepta, saying it, 'that you can't beat a millingterry man for a husband. Always a bit of gas of some description. Me own poor fellow carried me three times around Mountjoy Square on a Sunday night in the summer of 'nought three, to show me how he rescued Lady Smith in the Boer War. You remember him, Mrs. Brennan, ma'am?'

'Indeed and I do, Maria Concepta, and a fine presings of a
man he was too. Wasn't he, Mr. Cripping?'

'He was all that,' said Crippen. 'I heard said they were hard
set to make out whether he was the biggest dwarf or the smallest
giant in the whole of the Dublin Fusiliers.'

'Ah me,' moaned Maria Concepta, 'me dead hero. But go
on, Mrs. Brennan, ma'am, and tell us about poor ould Duck-
the-Bullet. Him and my poor fellow joined up together, having been let out the "Joy"[1] the one morning.'

'When he was half sobered up then, he'd tell poor Ace, the
wife, to cut off his head. "Here," he'd say, taking up the hatchet
that he was chopping up the furniture with, "take that in your
hand and say the words after me, and chop me head off. I
must have got a bad half off of Dewlaps last night, and I'm
too sick to wait for the market. Go on, Ace, cut off me head
when I tell you."

' "Duck-the"—that's what she called him for short, a kind of

[1] Mountjoy Prison.

pet name—"but I couldn't do the like of that. You'd be going around like Hanna Bow Lane with your head tucked under your arm." '

'Poor ould Duck-the-Bullet, I used to love the way he'd rend the marching song,' said Maria Concepta. 'I heard it the day meself and me own fellow got married.

'I'll never forget in the sacristy, me a bride and the groom so fine and fierce-looking in his red tunic and blue trousers and waxed moustache, and the priest lifting him up to kiss me and his pals of the regiment outside and they singing the marching song, led be poor ould Duck-the-Bullet.'

A frightening noise, like the cry of an out-of-work banshee, came from the lips of Maria Concepta:

> 'Oh, with your left right,
>   right about turn, this is the
>   way we go,
> Charging with fixed bayonets,
>   the terror of every foe,
> The glory of ould Ireland and
>   a thousand buccaneers,
> And a terror to creation
>   were
> The Dublin Fusiliers . . .'

She finished on a sigh: 'Ah! If only he was here to hear me.'
'Ah sure he's better off,' said Mrs. Brennan.
'You could say that again,' muttered Crippen.

Ahead to the sun from Lyons

*

WE LEFT LYONS early in the morning and drove on towards the sun. It was getting warmer. We went on through the
vineyards. I think grapefields would be a better description,
for they grew in rows and rows in huge fenceless fields, as
common as cabbage in Ireland.

Beautiful as it was, we lost interest in it after a while and only
wished to be woken up at a stop to get out, quench our thirst
and stretch our legs, for all the world like a Kerry All-Ireland
crowd on the long road to Croke Park, except that we were
silent and not so carefree. We had been the best part of two
days travelling and no matter how beautiful the destination,
man is not made for so much running around. Travel is a great
inducer of gloom.

The Belgian beside me agreed.

'No matter where you are you must take yourself with you,'
he said. The lady in front of us turned round and fixed a stern
look on him.

'Mine vife,' he muttered in English.

'*C'est ça*, mine vife,' said the lady superfluously and spoke
rapidly in Flemish.

'No, my love, I said I must take *myself* with me,' he said
very meekly. I do not understand Flemish, but so I thought he
said. They had not previously spoken to each other aboard the
bus.

She looked at him as much as to say, 'I know I had the
misfortune to marry the biggest eedgit in Belgium, but could

you not try and not demonstrate it in public, before half Europe?'

But just then the driver said we would see the Mediterranean over the hill, and she gave her husband a look as much as to say, 'My fine feathered friend, when I get you to myself in the hotel you'll know all about it,' glared at him, glared at me and turned to prepare herself for a glare or two at the Mediterranean.

It was as blue as I expected. We turned left as you go towards Italy, and just as they say about Killiney, there it was. Only like a stretch of fifty Killineys and the sun high in the heavens, stretching away to the left and Cannes all shining white, the sea one side and the endless tangled growth of the mountains going away into the Alps on the other.

There were camps and cars all the way in. The Parisian worker refers to the Blue Coast, the Côte D'Azur, by another name, which refers to the gang of international loafers, millionaire lay-abouts and royal bowseys that have made this place famous; but for a long way before we came to Cannes were camped along the road the tents of quite ordinary and no doubt respectable, French families; and the long-legged sunburnt youth of many nationalities, boys and girls, richer than any of the smart ones in their ten-pound-a-day hotels or on their luxury yachts, for they were young and healthy, and if the royalty and plutocracy had wealth at their side, these youngsters had youth.

'To hell with that for a yarn,' said the Belgian, 'what about them that has neither?'

Some people are never satisfied. I was glad when we reached Cannes.

'Good-bye,' said the Belgian, 'I go now vit my vife.'

'I'd sooner you nor me,' said I.

'Tank you,' said he. The wife told him to get looking after the baggage and glared at me.

I took heart of grace and glared back.

'Very good, I say good-bye for now.'

But I was not in such good fettle myself when I asked for a
bus to my destination and was told it was another twenty miles
away, back up on the mountains, and that a bus went within
four miles of it, but only once a week, and that was usually
yesterday.

'Come here,' said a policeman. 'I'll show it to you.'

He pointed up towards two or three hundred miles of
mountain, but being a stranger in the place I did not know one
Alp from another.

'Your road is up the Rue Carnot, turn left and keep walking.
About twenty-six kilometres. You can't miss it. Nothing else
up that way.'

'Only the wolves,' said I.

'No, not this time of the year.'

'Well, *merci, m'sieu l'agent. Au revoir.*'

'*Au revoir, m'sieu. Bonne courage.*'

'I'll need it.'

Terror in the Alps of France

*

I ALPED MY WAY, for some weary hours, till the sun went down and I found myself alone in the mountains and in the dark.

I remembered a book we had at school called *Seilg i measc na nAilp,* or *A Hunt in the Alps,* and when I saw a bright light appear and reappear in front of me, wondered with something approaching terror, as they say in books, whether I might be the object of this one.

A hoarse barking, as if in suppressed rancour and not all that suppressed, broke on my ears, and I started to run. But it was not much use running, for the light appeared in my path and the grunting bark grew louder, and anyway it was too far to run to Dolphin's Barn.

Not all the sins of my past life passed in front of me, but as many as could get room in the queue. Not since I slept in a barn at a place called Rambouillet, the other end of France, next to a horse that mended his own shoes in the small hours of the morning, was I so frightened.

I struggled on in this alien wilderness, and for company's sake thought of King Daithi, killed at the foot of the Alps. Why did not anyone ever warn both of us to keep out of them?

The light appeared again and the barking kept on, and it was better than a Mission. I sweated about seven pounds till a car came round the corner and caught me in the headlights.

It stopped and I never heard brakes go on with greater

pleasure. I mean, never with greater pleasure did I hear brakes go on. I was in no humour for worrying about my prose style at that moment. I didn't care if it was Dracula himself driving that heap of scrap, only to hear a semi-human voice and know there were other ways of communication beside this barking-grunting.

It wasn't Dracula—at least if it was he was not in uniform—but a man on his way home from work.

'*C'est le route à Montcolin?*' I asked.

He said it was the road to Montcolin and, what was better, that he would give me a lift to within a couple of miles of Montcolin.

'May your shadow never grow less, O man of the van,' said I with fervour and got into it.

I staggered into the Irish encampment, a villa high in the mountains, in the small hours of the morning, and was fed and given drink, and related my story. I spoke of the lights and the barking.

My host laughed.

'Those lights were fireflies. And the barking you heard was the grunting of the frogs.'

'Why, of course,' said I; 'how silly of me.' But I had never experienced anything the like of that on Sundrive Road.

Time heals all things and I woke up twelve hours later as good as ever I was.

We went down to Cannes by car and swam in the Mediterranean.

At Juan les Pins, Sugar Ray Robinson was performing in the Hollywood night-club, where a beer would cost you something in the region of a pound, if they sold you one, which they would if you were wealthy enough.

The usual drink is champagne, but I was told of an American in a hotel who wanted a cola with his lunch.

Colas are quite popular in France, but this hotel did not stock it, so a waiter was sent round the corner to buy one from a stall for fifty francs and twenty on the bottle.

The cola was duly bought and taken on a tray with ice and a napkin round the neck, to the gentleman, who drank it, expressed himself pleased with its quality, and cheerfully paid eight hundred francs for it (sixteen shillings), plus two hundred service, which made it the even quid.

The man that sold it to the waiter told me and he was told by the the waiter, when the waiter came back for the twenty francs refund on the bottle.

We went to our beach, which was called the Rio, and there, for the day, you could hire a seat and a parasol to shade you when you were out of the water, for a couple of shillings. You could get a quart bottle of iced beer for about one-and-nine-pence, and, best of all, you had the whole shimmering sea from there to Africa for nothing.

They also had for hire a kind of paddle-boat in which you sat and propelled yourself by a sort of pedal action on the same principle as a bicycle. I heard that people had tried to pedal to

Corsica on them, though why they weren't satisfied with where they were is beyond me.

Myself and a gang of kids, Irish, Anglo-Irish, Dutch-Irish and Russian-Irish, got in, and it would have taken a bayonet charge by the First Battalion to get us out.

There is no swimming till you swim in water like that. No breaking the ice. No diving in to 'put yourself out of pain' as we used to say in Dollymount. Just a matter of languidly rambling out till you are into it and alive again, after being comfortably comatose in the sun.

I cannot understand why very small children when swimming on your back, cannot get the idea of holding on to your shoulders, rather than half strangling you by the firm pressure of baby hands on your windpipe. Still, we enjoyed it.

I was more than repaid for the perils of the deep when I heard the smallest and most lethal one reply, when someone asked from the beach whether she wanted her big rubber raft: 'We don't want the wubber waft. We got Bwendan.' So she had, in a drowning man's grip, though I lived to tell the tale.

The best red wine

*

I DO NOT KNOW how it is that North Africa produces a *vin rouge* much stronger than anything from Metropolitan France. Because its inhabitants are mostly Mohammedan, and it is well known that The Prophet laid down a strict rule that his followers must not indulge in alcoholic liquids of any degree whatsoever.

It is called Mascara and is very cheap, even for France. It is sold mainly in working-class areas and costs twenty francs, about fourpence halfpenny for a little less than a pint, to drink in the café, though you can get it in a grocery for fifty francs the litre, which is one shilling a quart.

I had some in the Rue Cordelière, away in Port Royal in south Paris. This is where the followers of the Jansenist heresy had their headquarters. The monastery must have been a homely and jolly spot with the community assembled for their call-over of gloom, and debating whether the odds on damnation were more or less than a million to one on.

This is a slum quarter and indeed is said to be a 'tough' area and not quite safe for tourists. Dark tales are told in the cafés nearer the Champs Elysées of visiting English or Americans waking up in the gutter without passport or wallet, and any Arab quarter is regarded as unsafe.

I, however, have never in my travels met anything worse than myself, but then I don't know if they take me for a tourist. For the matter of that, I don't know what they take me for.

I had a friendly drink with North Africans in many a place and found them a decent, quiet-going people.

I know there are some hard chaws amongst them, and I would much sooner see the tinkers fall out at the fair of Aughrim than watch an Arab row.

On the Place Maubert, not far from the Boul' Mich' and just across the river from Notre-Dame, on a Saturday night I saw two of them get stuck into it. My life has not been a sheltered one, but I hope never to see another heave like it.

It was totally unlike anything I ever saw at home. Two Arabs came out of a restaurant, one of them rose his foot and kicked the window in, and having armed themselves with pieces of glass, they began slashing each other in complete silence, which to an Irishman made it a scene of incomprehensible horror.

Nor did the crowd which quickly gathered make the slightest attempt to interfere. They stood, casual and quiet, till the short double moan of the siren announced the arrival of the salad waggon, as they call the Black Maria, and then they scattered as the police jumped out.

But it's seldom enough one hears of, much less sees, rows like that, and even Marseilles is nowadays famous for the superb quality of its municipal architecture rather than for the ferocity of its apaches. Which is a word seldom used by the people it is said to describe.

I can understand that, for I remember a line by an English poet, recalling his alleged memories of my native city, in which he described:

> The ancient bowseys call their ageing mots
> Along the city wall . . .

And when I read this to one well qualified to bear the title from the antiquity of his bowseyhood, his only comment was a pious wish that the poet should go and get a Mass said for himself.

Even the slums in France have a quality of light and cleanliness that you do not find in the deserts of East London or the Gorbals, or Malpas Street for the matter of that.

And their youth are extremely well behaved to strangers.

In the Rue Cordelière the boys of the local *boule* club were celebrating the winning of some cup or league or other.

The only people over twenty years of age seemed to be their trainer and his wife.

They ate dinner together and then sat over the wine, codding the girls and codding one another over their girls, and then started a sing-song.

The songs they sang were mostly folksongs, though solo performances of the modern numbers in the style of M. Jean Sablon were well received, but it is a fallacy to believe that the empire of Hollywood and Tin Pan Alley extends to Paris. Most of these people had never seen a foreign picture in their lives, and could easily go through the rest of their lives without doing so. What makes an Irishman envious of the French is the *completeness* of their culture.

And when we talk of the stage-Irishman, we should remember that the world has been presented with a picture of forty million slinky-voiced Charles Boyers going around muttering about *l'amour* and throwing the national joyful optic at every woman younger than their granny, which is far removed from these people, hard-working all the week, but able to make a Saturday night of gaiety from the simplest ingredients.

By the way, I *don't* know what sort of a game *boule* is, or how it is played.

I wondered could it be the game beloved of Corkmen, which they call, around Gurranebraher way, 'bowels'?

Excuse my mistake

*

I WAS ON THE BOAT-TRAIN from France to Merrie England. And, to crown me, didn't I get a half-idiot of a fellow from some built-up bog of London called Tooting Bec or Balham's Ass, or some such, in the carriage with me, giving out the pay about the hardness of the French.

This means they took money off him for whatever they sold him, just the same as if he were not a Briton at all, but a Wog, or a Chink, or a Mau Mau. He talked about the nastiness of the wine, and how all that messed-up stuff they give you to eat couldn't be 'ealthy; and 'ow glad 'e'd be to get 'ome for a good cup of char, wouldn't you?

I replied frigidly that I was not going home. I was going to England, which was not my home.

'Well, excuse my mistake,' said he, 'but it's home to plenty of your people, isn't it?'

No attempt at repartee; he was just following the impulses of his big innocent Fulham Broadway head.

But it wasn't a bad retort, for all that. I became a little bit more disgruntled and began to see his case in a different light. Many of his countrymen had I met after the first few intoxicated nights around Pigalle, and finding out that one night of the Gay Paree act would cost him the whole of his holiday money, and the forlorn search for cheap, English-speaking company where they could all talk over their woes together.

An American tourist would have money, and the Irish, of the variety best known to me, would be happily absorbed in the problem of seeing whom they could do next.

Paris is not an expensive city by London or Dublin standards. It is very much cheaper if the tourist gets it into his cliggin that the laws of have-it-yourself-or-be-without-it apply there just as they do in most other parts of this sinful world.

But I have seen English people who would never dream of going to the Savoy Hotel or Claridge's for a drink, because they would know it was not for poor people, thinking they should be able to drink in the Crillon.

It's a hangover from the days 'when a pound was a pound' and every man could wallop his own niggers.

Even the meanest Englishman felt that abroad he was 'somebody', with a retinue of natives following him even unto the rickshaw door and screaming out in their quaint and monotonous chant, '*Baksheesh, baksheesh!*'

That dog is dead. It is fortunate for us now, that we never had any niggers to wallop, but were rather on the wrong end of the stick as far as walloping was concerned, because at least it saved us the pitfalls of the colonial attitude.

I have watched with admiration the almost occult efficiency with which a party of Irish pilgrim farmers could steer them-selves to a back-street bistro where they could enjoy the luxury of a good brandy at eightpence the nip. Talk about moving through the fair!

When the train pulled into Dieppe, I opened the offside carriage door and cleared the barrier like Shaggy Lad the live-liest day he ever saw, and into the nearest store.

This was formerly owned by a Limerickman, and any of Mac Lir's[1] waterfront clients that sailed on *Menapia* or *City of Antwerp* would have little difficulty in remembering it, for it is next door to the café of the redoubtable Mimi's.

Mimi's father had printed on his business cards: 'Me, Old Contemptible. Beer freezing cold, tea as hot as hell, just as Mother likes it. Café open 24 hrs to 24 hrs; shut for eating, Mondays. Up the I.R.A.'

[1] Mythological Irish sea-god.

This last was added at the behest of his clients of Cork, Ardglass, Clogher Head, Corporation Street and the Faythe, Wexford.

The boat was crowded for a cross-Channel boat, though to a survivor of the Holyhead run, it seemed as deserted as the Fifteen Acres on a Monday morning, but a man and woman sitting beside a vacant seat invited me to sit down.

'You could easily get your typewriter damaged,' said the girl.

'And besides,' said the man, 'we could get worse than a writer sitting beside us.'

It was a diabolical journey. Most of the people were sick and I was not feeling too good myself.

We stopped a few miles out of Newhaven and had an opportunity of examining the chalk cliffs of England for some two hours as the ship waited to get over.

Several times she took a run at it and stood up almost perpendicular, till she crashed back again and lay shuddering to collect her strength for another go.

A young priest from the West of Ireland discussed the matter in Irish.

'*Nior chuala mé trácht riamh ar raic ar bith ar an dtruip seo ach, is dócha,*' he finished cheerfully, '*gurab é sin an rud bhiodar á rá san* Princess Victoria.'[1]

'*Is dócha é,*[2] said I, at this stage of the game not caring whether we were wrecked or not.

But we were not, and my two friends insisted on giving me a lift to London in their car, where we could have a drink with themselves and a cartoonist on a London paper, who would also, they felt sure, enjoy hearing my views on their native land.

[1] 'I never heard before of any tragedy on this trip but I suppose that's what they were saying on the *Princess Victoria*.'
[2] 'I suppose so.'

How sorry they are to return

NOBODY enters or re-enters England with greater reluctance than the intellectual native of that country. Howard and Monica went down the gang-plank at Newhaven like early Christian martyrs. People have gone into Mountjoy with less reluctance.

For the matter of that, the intelligentzia of all countries is notoriously lacking in that sort of fervour that shows itself in frantic devouring of the old sod, to see if it tastes the same as it did on the way out.

Howard is a higher civil servant, and had finished a tour of British military establishments in various parts of the Continent. His wife went with him to keep him company and for the sake of the holiday.

We began a conversation on the way over from France. They asked me whether I intended to stay in England for long, and I told them I'd be there a couple of months. Monica wished to know if I knew it well. I said I knew a few places extremely well, without specifying what places.

Monica wanted to know if I liked living in England and watching with mounting distaste the white cliffs looming on the horizon, I did not like, for politeness' sake, to give her a straight answer. I said I thought my trip would be interesting.

But I need not have bothered. They both seemed to think that anyone of his own free will, leaving the Continent for England, must be more than a little mad.

After that we went down like a dinner with one another, and exchanged such pieces of cultural information as the story about the last words of Gertrude Stein, who sat up on her death-bed a couple of minutes before she died, and asked, 'What is the answer?' A second or two later she enquired, 'But what is the question?'

'Ah'd say she knows be this time,' said an Irish voice behind me. It was one of a band of students from Belfast I had met on the way over.

I left my northern brother giving grim consideration to these matters and went through the Customs with my friends.

For all they looted and robbed, the English made considerably less use of the swag than smaller imperialisms. The ugliness of most of London is unbelievable.

I was surprised to pass Piccadilly without noticing it, and Marble Arch is only about the same size as the Boer War memorial (known as 'Traitors' Gate') that they put up in place of Wolfe Tone's monument at Stephen's Green.

It is the second biggest suburb in the world, coming in length and breadth of built-up area considerably behind Los Angeles, which I am told extends for a hundred miles.

In the sense that I understand the word, the 'city' does not extend beyond the West End. A mile in any direction outside that, and so far as entertainment is concerned, at eleven o'clock at night you might as well be in Drimnagh or Ballygomartin.

Its people are kindlier, nosier and more respectable than any I have ever met.

The famed British reserve is as much a myth as the idea of the broth-of-a-boy Irishman, he of the ready wit and the warm heart and the great love for a fight.

Try it on the landlord or the grocer sometime. Tell him you'll give two rounds of the shillelagh in place of whatever you owe him and wait for the witty answer.

The landlord over here will know all about you if you remain with him for more than two days. And if it's a landlady she'll want to know more than that in twenty-four hours.

They also have an idea that most Irishmen go out in the morning and travel long distances by Tube to dig ditches for Lord Wimpey and Earl MacAlpine.

I was wakened at six o'clock on two occasions 'to go to work'. Luckily my accent, which I just discovered is as much of a 'brogue' as Barry Fitzgerald's, made unintelligible most of the flow of language with which the poor old one was greeted in the brightening morn.

Always I was met with the enquiry as to what I was. This was not meant in the Six Counties sense of Fenians or Orangemen, which political or religious curiosity I am beginning to think, is not the most troublesome kind.

What the landlady wanted to know was what was I in terms of the industrial effort.

I thought of saying I was a progress-chaser or a Power Samas operator, both of which occupations I have seen mentioned in

the newspaper advertising columns. But for both these occupations one must have false teeth and a taste for sausage rolls,
so I said I was interested in cattle.

She made further enquiry as to what part of the cattle
business I was interested in and I answered: 'Oh, steak, silver-
side, corned beef, brains, liver, heart, any part as you might
say, though I have never tried the nostrils. That, madam, I
am bound to admit.'

I am writing this in Bayswater, which is quite a pleasant
mid-Victorian suburb, one of the residential areas of the great
manufacturing bourgeoisie and now famous for its murders.

Mr. Christie had his private morgue just up the road in
Notting Hill; Flying Officer Heath's strangularium was across
the way in Gloucester Road. And the sink down which Haigh
poured numerous of his acquaintances is in a kitchen round
the corner.

The day is dark and grey, though brightened by a memory
of the wise and smiling south, like a flash of sun, a reminder
of the summer.

In Westbourne Grove, outside Lawrence's Store, he stood. A
stout little Italian, with a figure that owed nothing to privation
throwing out from the roots of him, and rising over the basses
of his own accordion, his splendid tenor voice: '*Ave Maria . . .
gratia plena.*'

O craft, thy name is Luigi! The strong West of Ireland
faces and the softer, smoother looks of French and Italian
smiled into one another, and navvies and waitresses, barbers
and busmen, Cork and Calabria, remembered their mothers'
people, it being Saturday and they out on the holiday prome-
nade, rewarded Luigi well for reminding them of it.

I'm back from the 'Continong'

*

LIKE MANY A ONE since 1950 I'm apt to say, 'I've just got back from the Continong.' Well, I have and I can tell you one thing and that's not two, that the weather in most of France was every bit as bad as you had here. I arrived in Calais and stepped off the boat on to six inches of snow, and more coming down.

Like the cute old sleeveen that I am where anything connected with drinking and eating is concerned, I decided it would be better to buy a bottle of wine and some comestibles, and eat it in the carriage, rather than trust to what the hawkers might present us with at the stops en route.

For on the third class from Calais, at this time of the year, they have no restaurant on the train.

On the Blue Train, of course, you could look in the windows of the Pullman and see the rich settling down for a banquet of some hundred of miles, and I've no doubt you could order anything from a live trout to a young child, if you fancied it and had the money to pay for it, or the money to go first class. But myself and my first wife were only on that route because we missed the Newhaven boat-train, which is cheaper and very comfortable.

I know Dieppe, Rouen and Dunkerque as well as I know Newry, Donaghadee or Drogheda, and Dieppe is a nice friendly place.

If you know how to do it you can dodge out under the train at the Gare Maritime—it's out in the street—and snake over to a wineshop and get cheese and *vin rouge*, and get back on the train again before you could say Lennox Robinson.[1]

There used to be a wineshop owned by a Limerickman and called the B.B.C. Wine Store.

They are very fond of third-class passengers in Dieppe, and at the height of the season the assmacrockery unloading the Rolls or the Daimler on the quay seem a little out of place, but Calais was not so well disposed towards the poor.

The town is so far from the quay that, setting off to look for my supplies, my first wife waved an almost tearful good-bye as I shuffled over the snowy wastes in my crêpe soles (thirty-two-and-six in Henry Street), looking like the late Rin-tin-tin going to do something very faithful. The town was too far away to get within an ass's bawl of a shop, so regretfully I trudged back after fifteen minutes in the blizzard.

But what a heartful welcome greeted me at the carriage window of my Calais–Paris express (via Amiens and Ville-cochon-sur-mer with a couple of dozen stops at intervening points to let old ones on with goats).

With what a heartfelt sigh of relief my first wife breathed down at me through the snow.

'Brendan, I thought you'd never come back.'

'*Oh, go raibh maith agat go deo, a ghrá, mar gheall ar an bhfailte lách sin.*'[2] I smiled, manlike. It may be that I owe that much that I have to go to Mass in a cab. What if I was unsuccessful in digging up some scoff for the trip?

Somebody anxious that I should come back. 'Your heart was in your mouth, thinking I'd be lost?'

'Well, you've got the tickets and the passports. I'd look well, I'm sure, left wandering round with no papers, looking for the price of a telephone call to the Irish Embassy from somewhere between Ameyens and Paris.'

'Amm-ee-ah.'

'What's that?'

---

[1] Lennox Robinson (1886–1958), well-known Irish playwright and Director of the Abbey Theatre, Dublin.

[2] 'Oh, thank you for ever, love, for that kind welcome.'

'Amm-ee-ah. The place between here and Paris.'

'It's Ameyens. A–m–i–e–n–s.'

'Yes, but it is pronounced "Amm-ee-ah". '

'Listen, if we ever get home and thaw ourselves out in the Gulf Stream well enough to walk, just try walking up to a Guard in Talbot Street and ask him to direct you to Amm-ee-ah Street Station!'

However, in the heels of the hunt we got to the railway station of Saint Lazare.

In the course of the next few days I showed my wife the Opéra and the Louvre. She said when I said, 'See that, that's the Eiffel Tower,' that her sight, thanks be to God, was not so bad that she would be likely to miss the tallest object in Europe at a distance of ten yards.

In return, when we did get home and tottered off the B. and I. and got three-quarters way up the North Wall, she brought me round the corner of Store Street and pointed. 'See that?' she asked.

I said I did.

'Well,' said she, 'that's Amm-ee-ah Street Station.'

Trails of havoc

*

'Brending Behing.'

  'Mrs. Brennan.'

  'How's Londing?'

  'Who?'

  'Londing. Didn't you come home from the Contingnent be Londing?'

  'That's right.'

  'Well, *came meal a vault yeh*.'[1]

  'What me?'

  'There's the Irishman for yous. *Came meal a vault yeh*—A hundred, thousand welcomes.'

  'Thank you, Mrs. Brennan, that's more nor civil of you.'

  'I'd a thought anyone would have known what "*came meal a vault yeh*" meant. Usen't it to be written up over the stage in the Queen's. Isn't that right, Mr. Cripping?'

  Crippen lifted his head from the unvarnished half of a pint tumbler and nodded, gloomily.

  'That's right. "*Céad míle fáilte*"; kindly remember you're not at home and do not spit; nor pass out tickets after the second interval; orange-sucking prohibited during cornet solo. But don't talk to me about London.'

  'Ah,' said Mrs. Brennan, feelingly, 'poor ould Crip, he's like that since the other day at the Curragh. Lester Piggott let him down for a three cross-double and the same back, anything to come first fav. at the other meeting.'

  'Thanks be to God,' said Crippen, 'he doesn't come over

[1] '*Céad míle fáilte.*'

more oftener. The short while he was here he done more damage than Cromwell or Willie Nevett. I'd *him* at the end of a length of accumulators the size of a summans in the Irish Two Thousand, and he let me down for one pound one and three (less tax).'

'Ah, sure, Mr. Cripping, that's months ago. It's no use keeping up a thing like that for ever,' said Mrs. Brennan. 'Better to forget it.'

'I can never forget it, and me with three pounds eighteen and threepence, less tax, going on to a two-to-one shot.'

'We keep the past for pride,' said I.

'Oh, he's like that this week past,' said Mrs. Brennan, 'and if you had have seen him in the shop when the result came in he was like a raging deming. Going round looking at the sheets and muttering, "Omagh, Armagh, Armagh, Omagh," like an incantating charm or smell, like what you're warned against in the Cathechissing. I don't think it's lucky.

'Still, Mr. Cripping, sup up, you're in your granny's and don't make strange. In honour of Mr. Brending Behing's safe return to his native vegigibble market. Concepta!'

An ancient, indestructible countenance, wrinkled and rugged enough to contain a shower of rain, but at present holding no more than the faintest traces of previous repasts of snuff, up-turned itself from the inside of a shawl. 'Mrs. Jewel and darling, did I hear you say something?'

'I've to go and watch me grandchild's eldest, the Lotty one, get a couple of skips of fruit over to me pitch, the butt-end of Moore Street. You know the pitch poor ould Funny Noises willed me?'

''Deed I do, the Lord have mercy on her, a good poor soul, poor ould Funny Noises. Still, she couldn't take her bit of Moore Street with her.'

'Still, and all, it was decent of her, and I looking for a bit of ground for me descendings. You might as well have a half in respect of her, not to mind Brending Behing being home, Me-Hall!'

'Yes, Mrs. Brennan, ma'm,' said Michael.

'Two pints of stout for the menkinds, and us ladies will have two half-ones and a bottle of Johnny-jump up.'[1] She turned to me. 'A surjing gave me the tip. Lovely man, he was. Only for the ould drop. Too fond of it.

'Man sent up to be operated on for an ingrowing toenail. Me poor surjing read the card wrong and thought it was a head amputating was required. Amputated the head, God love him, very severe operating, the patiengt never come out of it and the poor surjing was disgraced for life.'

'I knew one of them Swaines up in George's Packet, had his thumb amputated.'

'I remember them,' said Mrs. Brennan, 'they were married into the Leadbeaters.'

'That's right,' said Crippen, cheering himself up with a pull on his pint. 'Well, they were in a kind of religion that was very conscientious about the last day, and about getting up out of the grave, the way you were in this world. Well, Apollo Swaine . . .'

'Apollo?' I enquired.

'Yes, he got that name from hawking refreshments and shouting at the football matches, "Cigarettes, chocolate, toffee-app-oll-oh." Well, anyway, when he came out of the hospital he brought the thumb with him and gave a kind of a little wake for it in Jimmy-the-Sports' Bar up on our corner.

'Had it on the counter beside him, bringing it up to bury it. "I'm going to put it where the rest of me will be when I die," says Apollo. "A fellow would look well on the last day, running round the Nevin[2] like a half-thick and asking every-one, and they gathering up their ould traps themselves, 'Ech, did you see e'er a sign of a thumb knocking round?'"

'So we all agreed that there was a deal in what he said, and he invited us to the funeral of his thumb. We got up to the Nevin

[1] A particularly potent cider that was on sale in Ireland up to about ten years ago.
[2] Glasnevin Cemetery.

and buried it, and some was crying when the thumb was covered up in the ground, but Apollo mastered himself and gave a bar of a song before saying farewell.

'I can hear him this minute, and we all joined in with him when he sung out to his poor ould thumb, "And you will sleep in peace until I come to thee." '[1]

'Still, it wasn't like having a head amputating, having a tum amputating,' said Mrs. Brennan. 'When all is said and done, a body does have two tums.'

---

[1] Final line of *Danny Boy*.

We fell into the Waxies'
Dargle

*

'I'M FED UP and brassed off,' said Crippen, 'with the Continong.'

'I thought the extent of your travels was to the point of the
Wall,' said I. 'When were you on the Continent?'

'I'm gone blue melanconnolly from reading about it. Why
can't you write about something natural? Like the time we all
fell into the water at the Waxies' Dargle?'

'Or the time,' said Maria Concepta, 'the slaughter-house
went on fire.'

'Or, the Lord be good to us all,' said Mrs. Brennan, 'the
time the holy chap told us the end of the world was come to
Dún Laoghaire and we were all going to meet a watery end at
the butt end of the East Pier.'

'It's like the time,' said Maria Concepta, 'we seen the film
about the king and all the people stood up.'

'I'd have stood up for no king,' said Crippen crossly.

'You would,' said Mrs. Brennan, 'if you'd have seen this
one.'

'He was masterful,' said Maria Concepta, 'like me first
husband, who was only five foot nothing, but very stern.'

'Maria Concepta,' said Mrs. Brennan, 'give us that little
stave about the Waxies' Dargle.'

'Well,' said Maria Concepta, 'I'm not as good as I was the
time I took first place and silver medal at the Fish Coyle.'[1]

[1] *Feis Ceoil*: the premier Irish musical and singing competitions which are
held annually in Dublin.

'Ah, poor ould Fish,' said Mrs. Brennan, 'he wasn't bad when he had it.'

'Well,' said Crippen, 'give us the stave.'

'I will so,' said Maria Concepta, making a noise like a cinder under a gate.

> 'Oh, says my ould one to your ould one,
> "Will you come to the Waxies' Dargle?"
> And says your ould one to my ould one,
> "Sure I haven't got a farthing . . ." '

'God love your stomach,' said Crippen.

'Ahmen, O Lord,' said Mrs. Brennan, with feeling.

'Thank yous, dear faithful follyers,' murmured Maria Concepta. 'It maybe the last time I'll be singing at yous.'

'Thank *you*,' said Crippen . . . '*But there's them that says the divil is dead.*'

'Not half sooing enough,' said Mrs. Brennan, 'to hell with him.'

> 'And there's more that says he's hearty,
> And some says that he's down below,
> eating sugary barley . . .'

Maria Concepta finished on a low and throbbing note.

'That was massive,' said Mrs. Brennan.

'Not a diver in the Port and Docks could have got under that,' said Crippen.

'I would like, as you're the most melodious mezzo-soprano that ever muffled the markets,' said Mrs. Brennan, 'if you'd condescend to give us a verse of the *Zozzoligcal Gardings*.'

'Ah, the dear old days,' said Maria Concepta.

'Quite right,' said Mrs. Brennan, explaining, 'we both met our husbands in the Zoo.'

'Quite right, ma'am, and damn the lie,' said Maria Concepta, 'myself and my poor fellow'—she choked from emotion—'we met in the monkey house. And shared a bag of nuts with an orang-outang.'

'Well, carry on with the coffing, the corpse'll walk,' said Crippen, jovially, 'give us that bit of a bar.'

'I will so and the divil thank the begrudgers,' said Maria Concepta, 'with no more ahdo,' and without further ado she broke into a croak:

> 'I brought me mot up to the Zoo,
>   For to show her the lion and the kangaroo,
>   There were he-males and she-males of each shade and hue
>   Inside the Zoological Gardens . . .'

'My poor ould uncle—oney . . .'

'Owney?' I asked.

'Oney a marriage relayshing,' went on Mrs. Brennan. 'He

used to sing that. Till they buried him—after he died—in Kilbarrack. Out be Howth direction. That cementery is so healthy for dead people that if a live one had have went out there, they'd be there yet, and going on for all time, meeting themselves coming back.'

What are they at with
the Rotunda?

★

I WAS REARED a strict Dubliner. My father's people came
from the cul-de-sac (not a French word by the way, they call
it 'impasse') called 'George's Pocket' at the back of St. George's
Church in Temple Street, which is the most beautiful bit of
city anywhere.

My mother was born in Capel Street, and my father's
earliest memories were of his grandmother, a hardy old sort
from the lock-house on the Royal Canal above Mountjoy,
screeching in anguish to the chiming of the bells of St. George's,
'Oh, God forgive yous, there's the come-or-stays, there's the
come-or-goes, and yous wouldn't go as far as Wren's for the
little message?

'Get up, La; shake yourself, Boo; Christina, think of your
poor ould ma; which a yous, won a yous, any a yous, hurry
over there before Wren's is shut and get the little message.'

The come-or-stays were the chimes that rang at seven o'clock
just before evening service on Sundays and were so called because they were a hurried gathering of noise that seemed to say,
'Come to church or stay away, come to church or stay away.'

Though we were proud of St. George's, Johnson's jewel, of
which St. Martin-in-the-Fields is said to be an imitation, none
of us had ever set foot in it, and the main significance of the
chimes lay in the fact that besides calling sinners to repentance,
it also meant that the time was nearly 7 p.m. and the pubs
would be shut if La (Laurence O'Toole, an intimate friend of
one James Fitzharris, known to history as 'Skin-the-Goat')

133

or Boo, my grand-uncle or my grandmother, did not go with all dispatch and a gallon can for the 'little message'.

By the same token, if a native of this city may be permitted to mention *Ulysses*, Wren's is the pub occupied by Larry O'Rourke in 1904, on the corner of Eccles Street.

I have naturally some affection for the lovely Georgian Northside, but I hope when they rebuild Temple Street they won't do as they did with Gardiner Street and preserve a mock Georgian façade.

Let them tear the whole lot down and build new modern flats for the people.

It's easy enough to come over in your new Chev. from Mount Merrion or Foxrock, and have a nostalgic glance at the Dublin of Joyce and O'Casey before taking the visiting artist to Jammet's, but a bit of light and air would be more to the taste of the families to be reared in them.

The Wide Streets' Commissioners built well in their day for a class that only allowed the ancestors of the later inhabitants into their beautiful houses as servants. But let Ireland, building for its own people, do the best that modern technique can do for them.

God knows life is short enough without people wearing themselves out hauling prams round lobbies so that we can know what Hardwicke Street looked like in 1790.

Incidentally, the Hall there was the premises of the National Theatre before they moved to the Abbey, and was a drill hall for the Fianna before Easter Week, and, if I may say so, for long after. Con Colbert drilled in it and it was for long the headquarters of the Academy of Christian Art.

Once, interrupting a lecture by Father Myles Ronan just as he was about to reveal who pinched the Ogham stone outside Dan Murphy's door, I was the recipient of a stout box in the lug from that tough veteran George Noble, Count Plunkett.

I was the slowest mover of a pitch-and-toss school being held out in the yard, whose proceedings deafened the ears of the Christian Artists inside.

What I want to know, howsomeover, as they say in those parts, is what are they at with the Rotunda? The picture-house part I mean. Whatever it is, they shouldn't have been let. The stonework has been plastered over with some awful-looking substance that looks like granite-coloured glue.

I could see some sense in tearing it down and shoving up a new building if they wanted more room, but to leave it the same shape, covered with that stuff, does not seem such a good stroke.

If Pat MacNamara knows about it, wherever he is, God rest him, there'll be some choice blessings bestowed on the work.

Many is the time I saw him head the bill there, though I appeared on the boards of a rival house myself. Conscripted would be more like it. And a good many years ago now.

At that time there were three places running variety along 'Parneller'. There was the Rotunda, which also had pictures; there was the Star, opposite the Rotunda, and now a store for Aer Lingus; and there was the Torch, which was in Capel Street, the headquarters of the Dublin Trades' Council.

A relative of mine, a young married man of nineteen years of age, was knocking it out for the wife and family running a revue at the Torch. I was out walking with my father one evening when we met him and they adjourned for one.

The usual how-are-ye and is your granny still in the Union and all to that effect went on, and my father asks your man what kind of houses are they getting below in the Torch.

Your man shook his head mournfully and ejaculated one word. 'Shocking, diabolical, in the language of James Clarence Mangan, gapping. They're running a singing newsboy in the Roto, and a crippled singing newsboy in the Star.'

Even I, less than ten years old, standing in the corner supping me Vimto and glad to get it, knew what that meant in a district where everyone is a newsboy, an old newsboy, or the female relative of a newsboy. And a crippled newsboy. Sure, that'd leave them after the first verse with a lump in the throat you'd want to take to a blacksmith.

'But,' said he with a shake of his black head, 'Aughrim is never lost. We're not beat yet.'

'Be no manner of means,' says my old man. 'Have you booked Tetrissinny?'

'No, but I've the beatings of them.'

'A snake-charmer with Uileann pipes that can brush his hair with the sole of his foot, singing "You have me in a knot" at the one time?'

'I have a blind, crippled, singing newsboy.'

'That'd do them. If such a thing was to be had.'

'I have him here,' said your man, looking round.

I looked round, following his glance, but could see no newsboy, blind, crippled, or any other sort.

'Where?' asks my old man.

'Here,' says your man, putting his hand on my shoulder.

'Damn it,' says the old man, 'you wouldn't blind and cripple him for the sake of a week's engagement? Different if you were doing the grand tour of the thirty-two counties of Ireland and Newtownmountkennedy.'

I wasn't blinded or crippled, but the next Monday night saw me on the stage of the Torch, my few poor papers clutched to my side as I leant on my crutch and gazed upon the sobbing multitude through black glasses, balanced precariously on my one leg and my other strapped up to the small of my back, singing the *Blind Ditty*:

> 'Or the flowers that are so bright,
> I can hear sweet voices calling,
> And to me they are so kind,
> Bordsandbeesen flowers . . .'

I sang *Ramona, when day is done I'll hear you call,* for an encore, and *Oro, mo bháidín ag snámh ar an gcuan.*

After that I was billed as 'the blind, singing, crippled newsboy'.

The fun of the panto

*

'FUN with vulgarity' was the motto of our pantomime. It opened on St. Stephen's Night, feast of St. Stephen, and I never heard it called Boxing Day.

For long weeks before, the whole of the North Circular, from one side to the other, was a seething mass of intrigue and allying and counter-allying, crossing and double-crossing, that would have done credit to the United Nations, if such a thing had been going at the time.

At first it was the City side against the Croke Park side. Not all of these people knew one another, and indeed there were sore hearts in one street, which was highly respectable and in flats rather than rooms, at the thoughts of having to get up on the same stage as people from our street, but we had the good singers, and also, if we were not adequately represented we would not come, except to make trouble, and whatever our shortcomings in the matter of shut hall doors or prams and bikes in the hall, it was generally recognized that we were good at making trouble.

But by the time the rehearsals had started the quarrels and jealousies had reached an intensity that had ceased to regard any considerations of class or social position.

Many a life-long enmity was firmly founded on the question of whose little girl was to play a babe in the wood or whose big girl was to be a principal boy.

By the time the curtain was ready to go up, the hall was

grimly seething in a mood far too serious for anything so frivolous as fun, leave alone vulgarity.

The stewards were the subject of intense, whispered discussion, frequently libellous.

'Did you see who they had taking in the money in the one-and-sixpennies?—ould Baldy Conscience.'

'That's right. The same fellow used to go be the name of Sawdust Pocket when he was on the chapel door.'

'And sure if he's bad, the fellow who's with him is worse. They put the Boy Scouts on the door of the chapel while they were on holidays, and they got that much extra they never let them pair back.'

'It's up there on the stage they ought to be, giving a conjuring turn, now you see it, now you don't.'

'Sh-sh, the curtain's going up.'

The band played its opening bars and the girls went into their line number, singing one of many songs, all of which went like this:

'Oh, happy, happy, day and we hope you may
Enjoy our little show tonight,
That it may your heart delight, and make you merry and
    bright too-o-o-o-ni—ght.'

There was applause then from such of the audience as were personal supporters of members of the chorus. The rest waited for their own nominations to come out and contented themselves with a thin bringing together of the palms of the hands, but discreetly so as not to make noise. There was usually comment on the chorus ladies.

'I see that one of the Hegartys is out again. That blondy one there.'

The speaker's eldest daughter had been kept out of the chorus and a scalded heart will say many's the thing. 'I'd be long sorry to see any girl of mine got up in that get-up.'

'All the same, it's wonderful how she's able to get round the stage for a woman of her years. She's deserving of a diamond

jubilee presentation, I don't care what anyone says—forty years she's getting up on them boards. Oh, yous can laugh and sneer, jibe and jeer, but which of us would be that active at her age?'

Later in the show the court scene was in full swing.

Judge: 'How would you like your poor mother to be here and see you in the dock?'

Prisoner: 'Ah sure the bit of an outin' of the "Joy"[1] would do her good.'

In the audience, herself is putting himself through it for laughing, in burning, vitriolic whispers, till he squirms in the seat.

'You cur to go laughing at the red-nosed ruffian and his low jokes about the "Joy". Of course, you and him could shake

[1] Mountjoy Prison.

hands on knowing more about that place than most people—
and you hadn't as much as a grin on you when your daughter,
our own child, was up there singing *I wish I had a little cat*. But
wait.'

'Miss Eyelash Nick Gabbin—Nick I mean—she's a pain——'

A fierce jab of a programme in the ear attracts the attention
of the speaker.

'Who are you to call my daughter, *Eilis nic Gabhann*, a
pain?'

'I was only saying she was a pianist. That's what they have
her down here as. And I was only saying "Nick" is a funny
name for a girl.'

'You're only showing your ignorance of your own language—that's her name in Irish, *gan teanga, gan tir*,[1] you
perisher.'

A few nights later we'd be all out to get the paper and read
about it.

'. . . To introduce the various items there was the popular
Dublin master of ceremonies, Paddy (Whacker) Whelan. The
accompanists were Johnny Nola (piano) and Bill Gannon
(drums).

'The popular song *I like bananas, because they have no bones*
was a big hit, as was the song-scena with the sunflowers.'

---

[1] 'No language, no nation.'

It's Torca Hill for beauty

*

ONE OF MY TEACHERS was a young lady who was very refined.

This refined young lady teacher of mine came in one Monday morning and told us that she had spent the Sunday at Killiney.

'But,' said she, in tones of mournful refinement, 'it's ruined now with trippers. The place is full of them.'

Not knowing what she was talking about, but anxious to get in a bit of tee-hee before she'd ask me for an exercise that I hadn't done, I shot forward with fluent sleeveenery into the conversation.

'Ah, sure, teacher,' said I, 'isn't Dollymount the same, full of trippers. I was there yesterday with me da and me ma and Rory and Sean and Seamus and Brian and Dominic and Carmel in the pram, and it was rotten with trippers.'

'But Dollymount,' said my refined teacher, 'Dollymount is *for* trippers.'

I have never gone to Killiney since without thinking of her.

Sunday and Monday, I was out there. Looking out from the railway bridge at White Rock, along that curving beach and the wooded hills behind, it bears comparison with any part of the Côte d'Azur. Bernard Shaw said that the view from Torca Hill was so magnificent that no man that ever looked out on it was the same again. But the beach is not so good as at Portmarnock, or even at the strangely neglected seaside of Baldoyle.

Situate between Howth and Kilbarrack is the beach with the sea running up to the edge of the racecourse, and very convenient Billy Carroll the bookie says, for despairing fav. fanciers when the good thing drops dead a length from home.

Kilbarrack, my father always maintained, was the healthiest graveyard in the country, with the sea air. Last St. Patrick's Day on the way to the races I looked out for the Tricolour that used to wave over the grave of Volunteer Dan Head, killed at the Custom House. Never a funeral went out from the north side to Kilbarrack but the people would go over, after their own dead were buried, to gather round the flag and say a prayer for Dan Head. The ordinary people, without prompting from any organization.

And before I go back the other side of the bay to Killiney, I may tell you that in Howth they have a paper of their own, in which is reported the wedding of a girl from the Hill. The affair was carried out with function and capernosity, by all accounts, but my colleague from the *Howth Review* is not going to accept anything on hearsay. He says:

'The honeymoon is being spent in Minorca. (Understood to be an island in the Mediterranean.)'

I hope it was there when the happy couple got to it.

Now, to get back to Killiney. At the top of the hill, in a park maintained by the ratepayers, there is a peculiar-looking relic of the days when an eccentric and charitable landlord could indulge his dull fancies cheaply, by getting the people to build follies and wonderful barns, and get a good name for himself as a philanthropist at the same time.

This object has a marble inscription at the top which says:

'LAST year being hard with the poor, the WALLS about these hills and the ETC. erected by JOHN MAPAS, Esq., June 1842.'

JOHN MAPAS and his ETC. are bad enough, but could be left there as a curiosity and to remind the people of what our ancestors had to put up; but another notice is a standing piece of impertinence on behalf of the late Herrenvolk. It says:

'Victoria Hill.

'Acquired by the Queen's Jubilee Association Dublin, the 21st June, 1887, the day appointed for the celebration of the reign of Queen Victoria, 30th June, by his Royal Highness Prince Albert Victor of Wales.'

Well, we may deplore JOHN MAPAS's taste in ETC.s, but at least the building of it might have saved some poor creature from the Famine. Queen Victoria's good deed for the day, during her more famous famine a few years later, was the presentation of five pounds to the Relief Fund. It was said she gave another five to The Dogs' Home, Battersea the same day to prevent jealousy.

Turnip boat

*

FOR SOME REASON a friend of mine wanted to ship turnips
from a Six Counties' port. He wanted to ship anything from a
Six Counties' port because he wanted to sail into a British port
with a British Customs manifest, or whatever Mac Lir would
call it.

Our little ship was about the size of the Terenure bus. It
was eighty-six tons in weight or capacity, gross or net. Again
I leave it to the experts.

We sailed with a mixed crew. Some had been on a boat
before, and more hadn't. I was betwixt and between. I did
many's the trip on the *Larssen* and the *Royal Iris*[1] as a bona-fide
traveller, but had never actually rounded the Horn, or stifled
me mainbrace or anything of that nature.

The real sailors were the Skipper, the mate, and fireman.
The rest of the company were merchant adventurers along
with the owner, and I was a merchant adventurer's labourer,
so to speak.

The real sailors slept forrad, and we had accommodation
aft, where, as Sammy Nixon said, villainy could be plotted in
peace.

Sammy came aboard wearing rather tasty pin-striped kid
gloves, and a Windsor knot of some dimensions. His hat he
wore on the Kildare side, even in bed, for he had not a rib
between him and heaven.

He had come straight from a pub in Belgravia, flown to

1 Dublin Bay paddle-steamer.

Collinstown, and after a stop for refreshments in Grafton Street, or thereabouts, had come down by taxi to the North Wall, where he had her tied up.

Sammy had never been on a boat of any description before, and till he had heard from Eddie, thought they'd been done away with, like the trams.

'Muscles' Morgan, his china, was due on a later plane, and what old 'Muscles' would say when he saw this lot Sammy did not know.

'Muscles' when he arrived dressed in the same uniform as Sammy, all eight stone of him, said: 'Corsalawk, e'n it? Lookah er, Namber One, cock,' which he repeated many times during our subsequent voyages, and Eddie, Sammy, 'Muscles', and I retired aft to drink rum, like sailors.

The sailors we left forrad, brewing their tea, darning their socks, winding the dockwatch and with infinite skill, putting little ships into bottles. There would be no shortage of bottles. Before we thought of calling the skipper we already had a couple of empties for the little ships to be put into them.

The Skipper fell to our level, through drinking, gambling and sniffing. Just common sniffing. I am not unacquainted with the national catarrh, but he was a most hangdog-looking man, with a sad puppy's face pleading for a friendship, or at least tolerance, and his shape and make was that of a Charles Atlas in reverse. And the whole world of ineffectual weakness was in that sniff.

Eddie picked him up in the West End, and brought him over with the boat.

He sniffed nervously to me that he had never been in Ireland before, though his family had a house in Mount Street, and if I possibly thought, if it would not, sniff, be too much, sniff, trouble could I, would I not, presuming on our short acquaintance, tell him how to get there? His father was born in it.

Better than that. I would bring him to it. And did, after a couple of stops at other points of interest on the way. And he cried and sniffed, and when I stood him with his back to Holles

Street Hospital, he looked up along Fitzwilliam Square and Fitzwilliam Place, lit by the sun on the mountains behind the long range of golden Georgian brick, and wept again, and said there was not the like of it anywhere else.

So I got Eddie to call him down, and he sat in a corner and apologetically lowered an imperial pint of rum and hot orange. I think he took a subsidiary couple of rossiners to make up for the orange.

For if it's a thing I go in for in a human being it's weakness, I'm a divil for it. I thought of the Katherine Mansfield short story, where the *Daughters of the Late Colonel* are afraid of the old chap, two days after his funeral, leaping out of the linen press on top of them, and one of them cries: 'Let's be weak, oh, please, let us be weak.'

He even sniffed an apology to 'Muscles' and Sammy for their seasickness the first two days out, while they lay in their death agonies and shuddered from the cup of rum he would minister unto them.

147

He lowered it himself and weakly took himself up on deck to look for the Saltees. We had a reason for going to France, before the Six-Counties manifest would be of use to us.

When we came back for our turnips, the final arrangements had to be made with what I will call the Turnip Board, and we marched up the main street of a northern port on Armistice Day.

Eddie went into a shop and came out with two big poppies. I shook my head.

'No bottle?' said I, in his native language.

'None of this old mallarkey,' said he, 'there's a reason why I must get a cargo of turnips off these geezers.'

'That's not what I mean. They won't fancy poppies.'

'This is "Northern Ireland", 'nt it? They're for the King and Queen and all that lark, 'nt they?'

'Not here. This is "Southern Northern Ireland".'

Eddie sighed. 'Only a nicker wasted,' and dropped his two ten-shilling poppies in the gutter. 'I get on. Mostly R.Cs. here, eh?'

We met the chairman of the Turnip Board in an hotel and Eddie shook him by the hand.

'I think it's an 'orrible shame the way, the way these Protestants treat you 'ere, Mr. MacConvery.'

Mr. MacConvery's plum face turned blue, and his stomach went in and out at a hell of a lick.

'The cheek of you,' he croaked; 'my old friend,' he indicated a little man like an undertaker's clerk sitting nearby, 'Mr. Macanaspie, respected member of the Presbyterian community, vice-chairman of the Turnip Board, we have it one year, they the next, chair and vice, turn an' turn about . . . I . . .'

His indignation collapsed for the want of breath, and I got a chance to explain that it was a joke, and it gave Eddie a chance to tell how he'd taken a prize in the Band of Hope himself.

And in the heel of the hunt we got the turnips and some months later, in the bar of the Latin Quarter, as us old sea-dogs hove to in there, Eddie remarked that Partition was strategically useful.

Red Jam Roll, the dancer

*

I AM REMINDED of boxing matters by an encounter I had this day with a former opponent of mine, pugilistically speaking. I do not mean that our encounter this day was a pugilistic one, but it was pugilistically speaking we last spoke. And that, at the lane running alongside the railway end of Croke Park.

Our street was a tough street, and the last outpost of toughness you'd meet as you left North Dublin for the red brick respectability of Jones's Road, Fitzroy Avenue, Clonliffe Road, and Drumcondra generally.

Kids from those parts we despised, hated and resented. For the following sins: they lived in houses one to a family, which we thought greedy, unnatural and unsocial; they wore suits all the one colour, both jacket and pants, where we wore a jersey and shorts; they carried leather schoolbags where we either had a strap round our books or else a cheap check cloth bag.

Furthermore, it was suspected that some of them took piano lessons and dancing lessons, while we of the North Circular Road took anything we could lay our hands on which was not nailed down.

We brought one of them to our corner and bade him continue his performance, and thereafter any time we caught him, he was brought in bondage to the corner of Russell Street and invited to give a performance of the dance: hornpipe, jig, reel, or slip jig.

This young gent, in addition to being caught red-footed, was by colouring of hair red-headed, and I've often heard since that they are an exceedingly bad-tempered class of person which, signs on it, he was no exception. For having escaped from his exercises by reason of an approaching Civic Guard, by name 'Dirty Lug', he ran down to the canal bridge which was the border of our territory, and used language the like of which was shocking to anyone from Russell Street and guaranteed to turn thousands grey if they hailed from some other part.

However, our vengeance for the insults heaped upon us by this red-headed hornpiper, that thought so bad of giving the people an old step on the corner of the street, was not an empty one.

One day, not alone did we catch him, but he'd a jam roll under his oxter—steaming hot, crisp and sweet from the bakery

—and the shortest way from Summerhill to where he lived was through our street. He was tired, no doubt, with wearing suits and living in a house with only his own family and carrying that heavy leather schoolbag, not to mind the dancing lessons; no doubt he thought he had a right to be tired, and he took the shortest way home with the cake for his ma.

He could see none of our gang, but the fact that he didn't see us didn't mean we were not there. We were, as a matter of fact, playing 'the make in' on Brennan's Hill down by the Mountjoy Brewery when his approach was signalled by a scout, and in short order 'the make in' was postponed while we held up the red fellow and investigated his parcel.

We grabbed the booty, and were so intent on devouring the jam roll that we let the prisoner go over the bridge and home to plot his vengeance.

He was a hidden villain all right. Long weeks after, myself and Scoil (or Skull, have it any way you fancy) Kane were moseying round Croker, not minding anything in particular. Kerry was playing Cavan in hurling or Derry was playing Tyrone in anything, but it wasn't a match of any great import to any save relations and friends, and a dilatory class of a Sunday afternoon was being had by all, when the Scoil (Skull) and myself were surround by a gang, if you please, from Jones's Road, and who but the red-headed dancing master at the head of them.

But we didn't take them seriously.

'Sound man, Jam Roll,' said I, not knowing what else to call him.

'I'll give you jam roll in a minute,' said Jam Roll.

'You're a dacent boy,' said I, 'and will you wet the tea as you're at it?'

'Will you stand out?' says Jam Roll.

'I will,' said I.

'In the cod or in the real?'

'The real,' said I; 'd'you take me for a hornpiper?'

He said no more but gave me a belt so that I thought the

Hogan Stand had fallen on me. One off the ground. The real Bowery Belt.

'Now,' says he, when I came to, 'you won't call me Jam Roll again.'

'You were wrong there, Jam Roll.'

Flowers are safe at
Dolphin's Barn

*

IF I GOT MY HANDS on whoever made it up I'd give him 'Bimbo'. It's bad enough having to do the work before you get the money, without having 'Roley-Poley-Oley-Oh' bawled at you from every house in the block. It penetrated the oak panelling of my spacious library and drove me out to vote.

In the hot sun, Corporation painters were burning off sashes and hall doors at the rate of a mile a minute. If anything could cheer up that mysterious body the ratepayers, their hearts may rise with the information that the squad decorating municipal property this year are as fast and efficient a gang of painters as ever I've seen.

The painters themselves, like everyone else that lives in a house, are ratepayers. With a small 'r' because they don't, as Cyril Connolly would say, 'make a thing' about it.

Newspaper columns sometimes carry a sarcastic note on the navvy straightening his back and taking ten full seconds over it, all unconscious of the scribe taking notes from the snug window opposite; and the cleanest, jolliest fun, round the suburban breakfast table, is excited by Papa's reading out from the morning paper a bit about a hole at the corner of Grafton Street and some good-humoured chaff at the expense of the chaps at the bottom of it.

Coming out of the voting, I passed over the canal on the way in to town. The grass roundabout on the corner was a vivid green and, to tell the truth, I don't know what else to call it.

The important thing was the blaze of scarlet flowers in the centre. There was neither guard nor railing protecting them, and the little children played round and about them, while their mothers and big sisters knitted and chatted on the edge of the roundabout. And the flowers as safe as the orchids above in the Botanic Gardens.

Now roundabouts and grass plots at the edge of Greater Dublin pavements have been put down before, and walked over before the grass got a chance of shoving itself up, much less flowers, and I think I know the reason this one at Dolphin's Barn Bridge survived when others didn't.

It is raised on a stone base three feet high.

Now few of us can take a leap like that in our stride, whereas it requires a conscious effort of will to walk round, rather than over, a space on a low cement coping almost level with the ground.

Like the apple trees that greet you on the roadsides of north

Wexford, the unguarded scarlet glory at the Barn Bridge are a pledge to the dead that our slanderers were liars.

The coy carry-on of the women voters was worth listening to on Election Day.

Two elderly women, who have voted for opposing parties since women got the vote, walk over together to the schools.

'Ah, sure, Julia, it's like what poor Dan O'Connell said——'

'The Lord have mercy on him,' said Julia, politely.

'——to the man he met on the road. This man was breaking stones, and he asked Dan who was going to get in. "Whoever gets in," said Dan, "you'll still be breaking stones." '

'Ah, sure, isn't it the truth for you, Maria?' said Julia. 'I have to go over here, at the other door. I'll see you when we come out.'

'I'm glad to see you so united in your politics,' said I.

'Is it me be united with that one? Sure, she's gone over to give her one, two and three to the other crowd. Pity she wouldn't break her neck, and God forgive me for saying it, before she got to the ballot-box; but I'd never blame her for being always the one way, and her ould one a scrubber in the Vice-Regal.'[1]

And when she came out: 'Ah, there you are, Mrs. Jewel, I was just waiting on you. I was just saying to this chap here, "Isn't the day very changeable. You wouldn't know what to pawn." '

---

[1] The Vice-Regal Lodge. Residence of the *ci-devant* Lord Lieutenant.

On the road to Kilkenny

*

'DID YOU EVER SEE a stuffed Derby winner?' I asked. 'If ever you go to Kilkenny look out for the Hole in the Wall; you'll get eggs there a dozen a penny, and butter for nothing at all.'

'Thanks be to God,' said Crippen, 'it's not the one way we all go mad.'

'Or did you ever see a fighter aircraft on the side of the Naas Road?'

'Well, it must have been an awful thing for your poor mother to be looking at you, when she came to the reeleysayshing that you were gone round the bend,' said Mrs. Brennan.

'Tell us,' said Crippen, 'is it long since you went mad?'

'Were you ever in a village with ne'er a pub?'

'Now, here,' said Crippen, 'don't be giving us that—stuffed Derby winners, aeroplanes on the side of the Naas Road. What will you think of next, and tell us you saw it?'

'Well, John Devoy's little cottage just outside of Kill. And the huge motor assembly plant just outside the city, and the Irish-American drainpipes' plant farther on.'

All this I saw on the road to Kilkenny, ye faire citie, the other day.

I'd say the motor assembly people should be as welcome as the flowers of May; they bring Continental technique and a width of ideas as wide as Europe to our shores.

As we proved in the cases of aviation and electrical engineering, our people are not bad at the catching-on business, but it was sad to see the best and biggest fields in the hands of the foreigner.

I would not be the instigator of animosity toward anyone, no matter what their class or nationality, but it's easier for the foreigner to buy an acre of Ireland than a foot of France.

If the people take advantage of that and the lower taxation, I don't see how they can be blamed; but you have political parties and armies and leagues, all claiming that their particular brand of patriotic craw-thumping is best designed to undo the conquest, and here is the very heart of Ireland in alien hands.

I saw, on the way through Carlow, bigger fields than I knew existed in this country, all in the hands of big people from another land.

I thought of the patient toil of the Aran people to make a little bit of ground with sand, seaweed and sweat, and remembered the weary faces set to the Liverpool boat, and thought of an old song of my grandmother's:

> 'Yes, yes, 'tis a dear little pot of it,
> Yes, yes, 'tis a dear little isle. . . .
> Now, come on and rise, every man of you,
> Now is the time for a stir to be made,
> Ah, Paddy, who made such a lamb of you . . . ?'

And as regards four-fifths of the country there is no need for guns or pikes to adjust the situation.

You could look for miles and not see anything but the roof of the next big house, and nothing except animals on the broad acres in between, and there I thought of the little houses set nearly back to back round Carraroe.

I walked under the trees that shaded Rinuccini in the city of Kilkenny, and sampled the ale. I stood on a bridge under the Castle, and looked in the fat and sluggish river.

The man I was with described it well when he said that Kilkenny city is a place unto itself.

We were standing in the hotel, nourishing ourselves, and this prosperous-looking individual, on being introduced to me, asked me what I was.

I said I was a writer, but later on got the telling of it from the man I was with.

'What do you mean,' says he, 'saying you're a writer? I've to do business with that old fellow and let on to be a bit respectable. I told him you were an unemployed painter.'

I was only a minute in Castlecomer, but the next chance I get I'll stop longer. It's a darling, sturdy, sizeable town, and plenty of jizz about it. The coalmines are not far away and Wolfhill only the bawl of an ass from it.

I liked the looks of the people, and for the short while I was there relished their chat.

A miner who was waiting on his wife to finish her shopping pointed down to an elderly, very correct-looking man, wearing a black suit and a butterfly collar, and savouring a drop of gin for himself.

'That's the Boxer down there,' said the miner.

'The boxer,' said I, wondering at the vagaries of the fight business, and Nel Tarleton from Liverpool winning a British Empire title with only one lung, and after being rejected as unfit for service with the British Navy.

This old chap looked like the hard collar was holding him up and had a pair of shoulders like a naggin bottle.

'Well,' said I to myself, 'the wind bloweth where it listeth.'

'The boxer,' said I.

'That's right,' said the miner, 'that's what he's known as in ——,' mentioning the place. 'When that fellow puts you down you stop down.'

'Goodness gracious,' or words to that effect, said I, 'you don't mean he's still at it?'

'Bedad he is,' said the miner. 'He's left a couple in the cemetery this very morning—he's the undertaker in them parts. That's why they call him the Boxer.'

A word for the brave
conductor

*

THERE IS SOME CONNECTION between Donnybrook and
the Zoo.

Old and respected resident: 'What do you mean, you cur?'

The Number Nine and Number Ten buses. I saw the time you
could go from John Reddin's to the very gate of the Phoenix
Park and have change out of a pound.

For the next few days we will be thinking of the increases
in the bus fares, and will continue to feel a twinge every time
we part with the extra few coppers a day, till something
else goes up and we've got used to the new bus fares, because
we're too busy moaning about the rise in the price of something
else. And quite justifiably so. But not at the conductors, I hope.

I do not set up as a paragon of good civic behaviour, but I
was very annoyed a few days ago to hear a most respectably
got-up lady giving out dog's abuse to a bus conductor because
she had gone past her stop.

She may have made the genuine mistake of thinking she had
told him where to let her off—as a matter of fact she had said
nothing to him beyond grunting when he gave her ticket and
change—but even so her manner was that of an ill-trained dog
suffering from a bad dose of hydrophobia.

She went off in the direction of the canal, still barking and
yapping, but to herself.

I'm sorry to say that all of us are inclined to be unreasonable
with public servants, who are, after all, not paid to be public
doormats.

We come late for an appointment and expect the bus should be just there as we go to the stop. We wait a bit, and one of these querulous individuals that goes in for such port becaus it's cheaper than talking in public houses, opens the betting with a remark that it's always when you want a bus that there's never one there, and getting well into it now, that them fellows don't care if the people froze to death along the route, while they were lounging there at the terminus smoking and chatting.

Then an acid-toned mezzo-soprano joins in: she doesn't know what these people are coming to these days, but when the public are willing to put up with it, etc., till the bus comes and the unfortunate conductor, before he has a chance to even ask for the fare, is glared at by such a double line of Draculas and Frankensteins, that you'd nearly be demanding horror money for having to look at them at all.

At rush hours in the city, it's hell open to sinners on a wet night if a conductor dares to regulate the stampede from the queue.

True, it's no nice thing to go home in damp clothes, but it's not the conductor's fault if the bus only holds a certain number of people. As I heard one remark to a man trying to force his way on a well-loaded bus, 'Hey, Mac, it's not made of rubber.'

Dustmen, too, are a breed of citizens that well earn their six and a half quid.

People putting the most shocking kind of debris into their bins are a hazard, but the Irish people, whatever their faults, have great natural cleanliness and self-respect, and that is not the worst source of extra annoyance to the fellows in the cleansing department.

They tell me themselves that they mostly fear makeshift bins with jagged edges. It doesn't take much imagination to picture the chances of getting a savagely infected cut across the palms in their business.

Then, of course, I must not leave out the most pestilential of my own nearest and dearest and next-of-kin—the professional 'Dubalin' man.

Your gills that can't go on a bus, into a post office, or stand in front of a bar but he's looking for 'bogmen', like Cromwell sniffing for papists. His ear detects an accent from beyond the Pale, and then woe betide the young man or woman that fumbles with a stamp or spills a flat pint. How many a tear was cried in lonely digs during the first week up, after a few nasal jibes about 'the counterrymen' from this snuffling catarrh player?

His good woman, 'th' oul' mot', Madame Catarrh, is not far behind him in her seeking out of the native strain in people. Though her standards of 'Dubalinism' are severer, going back Nordic fashion to the immediate ancestors.

Like the old lady I heard discussing the return of a friend of mine from the golden-gloves boxing tournament in Chicago where he had won a title.

'Deh hung ous a banner for him, so deh did, the bewzivul

banner we had over from the Congress with St. Patrick with green whiskers riding on a bewziful snake, the faz of a bullig eh was, like he was a saint or sumpthin, and sed "*kayed meela vawicha*", a hundred touzand welcomes and yer a credit to deh cizzy and sure hees not a cizzy fella at all, hees mudher was a Monster——'

'A what?'

'A Monster woman—from Monster down in Cork iz iz—like Ulzter—oney diz *iz* Monster, have you me? The counterry iz iz—dere y'are now sez I, all dat come motion over a counterryman, an now err one deezan Urrishmen going round an noz a word aboudem.'

Snow through the window

*

I SAT DOWN this morning after a kipper, some mushrooms, cheese, black coffee with bread and marmalade and butter, and looked out of the window, thinking of the poor.

While the turf was blazing itself into a white heat of fragrant caressing warmth, I digested my breakfast and reflected on the excellence of my condition.

'The wicked,' I thought happily, 'prosper in a wicked world.' But, alas, not the worst of us is free from the improving influence of a good woman. My first wife came in and said, 'I thought you were doing that bit of an article today?'

I looked out the window again and shuddered.

'You're not expecting a man to work in that kind of weather?' said I, with a look at the blizzard.

But she was adamant and pointed to this masheen, as the man called it, and I only got out of the house by a mutter about a telephone call to be made from Peter's. I reflected during my hundred yards battle through the snow that if the Corporation would not build a tunnel from our house to Peter's, I'd have to get my overcoat out of pawn.

I may say that the height of good humour prevailed in this igloo of ours.

There were elderly ladies of a loyalist nature from Ballsbridge, and pensioners from the Indian Army. There were former ladies of the Sweep, two Mayo chaps off a building job on Wet Time, a deported American and a couple of African medical students, a man that sold pigs the day before yesterday, a well-known builder and a publican, equally well known in his own shop, myself and Packy from Scarriff. There were some English people over for a holiday in Peter's and a man who used to stop greyhounds for a living.

Now, it is not to be thought that we were not thinking of those less fortunate than ourselves that were stuck out in it. Nor is it to be implied that we thought lightly of the sufferings of any worker in bad weather, from the docker trying to graft over the freezing water to the man chasing a ewe up the sides of Tón-le-gaoith in the County Wicklow. But it was the way we were looking out the window and counting our blessings for ourselves.

And, as is the case in times of general dislocation, there was, as I said, the height of good humour, like what Raftery described at Galway Races:

Bhi sluagh mór daoine ann, from every airt and part,
Siad deas mácanta, croidhiúl ann, and singing with a good heart,
Ag rinnce is ag órdú dighe, ag gabháil an 'Cruiscín Lán',
The day we spent in Paul's house, *maidin a' tsneachta bháin*.

That's not what Raftery wrote, but it's as well as I can remember, and go and write one of your own if you think you can do better.

I heard it told there, as the first of a series of lectures that should be entitled 'We'll neither work nor want', the story of a man that had a slight accident in a very great industrial concern.

Your man has this accident and is laid off for a week or so, and then he comes back to be examined by the company doctor.

'But there's only one little thing,' says the doctor. 'Just a teeney weeney bit of bone. A splinter and no more, only it's aimed straight at your heart. We'll have it out in no time.'

'You will,' says your man, 'in my eye.'

'Ridiculous,' says the doctor. 'It'll only be a very slight operation, a matter of a couple of days in bed to extract this bit of bone—but,' and he calls for two minutes' silence, as these fellows will, when they're out to put someone through it, 'if you leave this little bit of bone in you it's going straight for your heart like a torpedo.'

'That little bit of bone,' says your gills, 'I make me own arrangements about, and you're not operating on me.'

The doctor sighed, and the next week your man was out on full pension, which they gave him cheerfully enough, as he wouldn't live more than a week or two to draw it, with that little bit of bone in him.

The week he got the pension he went into hospital and had the bone taken out, and last week threw snowballs at the passers-by as he waited to draw the one thousandth and eighty-sixth weekly instalment of his pension.

Something like the boneman's stroke would suit me down to the ground and keep me in out of the elements these cold days.

I was reared a pet, God love me.

Swine before the pearls

*

I READ THE MIDDLE PAGE of the Irish edition of the *Sunday Express*, which was given over to the Beaverbrook prophet resident in this city. It was an article about Eamon de Valera and so full of '. . . smoke and stars', '. . . the dour black porter of the Celt', '. . . a Machiavellian mind for statesmanship', '. . . myth, mystery and legend', and Chinese laundry-keepers and even loyal sons of St. Patrick, as to make one wonder whether its author is not in grave danger of meeting himself coming back.

There is more gas with the locals on the rest of the paper. Get on this, for instance; a letter to the editor.

I read in the 'Sunday Express' last week, that a woman fell into the Victoria Memorial fountain when the Queen was on the Palace balcony. I was that very wet person—or rather, one of the two who went in.

But who cared? I had seen our Queen and to see her was worth getting wet and an hour's journey home to dry clothes.

(Mrs.) D. L——, N.9.

Mrs. L——, fifty-one-year-old nurse, has been in love with royalty as long as she can remember. She has seen two Coronation processions, three Lyings-in-State, and most public functions attended by royalty during the last forty years.

The scribe, on the same page, has been hearing about the masque which undergraduates will stage for Princess Margaret's visit to the Oxford women's college, St. Hilda's.

The masque Porci ante Margaritan *has been specially written for the occasion.*

The Princess will be greeted as 'Fairest of pearls, the world thine oyster', and will hear her astrological future foretold as:

'Perhaps you will be meeting someone new,
Romance will very likely come to you.
Perhaps you will antagonize a friend,
But make it up, most likely, in the end.'

Miss Mann, principal of the college, saw the script and sent it to the Queen Mother. It was approved.

Translated, the masque's title is: *Swine before a Pearl.*

'My first was the very same. Poor Gonzaga Ignatius, "Hogger" I called him for a pet name,' said Mrs. Brennan. 'Lost in the Boer War and never found. Lovely fellow, wasn't he, Maria?'

'Not tall enough to pick shamrock,' muttered Maria.

'All the same he was lovely in his little pillbox cap and his doaty little face with the big black moustache. You could nearly lift him up by it. And he was the very same about swine. Swine before pearls, or diamonds or anything.

'He'd get up in the middle of the night to eat swine, from the crubeen to the tip of the left ear.

'Swine before a pearl. Or before a pint. You couldn't beat his little hands away from this counter till he'd sunk twenty of them after a feed of pig's cheek.'

'God be with the days you'd get a head for two shillings and only newly married couples got a cheek between them,' sighed Maria.

'It's well I remember it,' said Mrs. Brennan. 'Why wouldn't I and I married and a widow before I was eighteen.

'I was the champion widow of the quarter and if there was a widow's five-furlong sprint I'd have won it, with a length in hand, fifty years ago. For a long time I was betwixt and between, of course. Not knowing whether I was in it or out of it.'

'So?'

'And more so, Brending Behing. The War Office had no news of him for weeks, and thought he might have been a prisoner, and still alive. Though, in the heels of the hunt, we gave up all hope.'

She sniffed into the butt end of the tumbler.

'Ah, yes. When they found six Dubling Fusiliers' buttings in a lying's dem.'

'Them lions,' said Maria. 'You could never trust them.'

'And there was boings with the buttings.'

'Buttons and Bones,' said I.

'That's it,' said Mrs. Brennan. 'Once they got the buttings and the boings, and God help poor little "Hogger", you'd have known his boings anywhere, they fixed me up with me pension.'

'Perhaps *you* will be meeting someone new,' I quoted.

'Ah, don't be talking. Didn't I meet him coming out of the 1906 Exhibishing? Just leaving the native village he was, after leaving two dozen of large bottles and a quarter of brawn for the chief of the Royal Izumbis, and Earl of Addis Ababababa, a chap be the name of Hogan, from Malpas Street.

'His father was a chef in O'Keefee's, the knacker's. Oh, indeed and I did meet someone new. Just like the man says in the poing.'

'I wrote a poem one time,' said Crippen.

'I wouldn't doubt you,' said I.

'And indeed I'm sure and you did, Mr. Cripping, and it wouldn't be your best.'

'Say a bit of it, so,' said Michael, from behind the counter.

Crippen glared angrily round, as poets do, and shouted, 'And sure, there yous are again, tormenting and annoying and persecuting me, all because I trust a bit of me heart's core, a part of me pain, a bit of meself, a moment of me experience, pinned down in its trembling torture to the paper, like a butterfly to the board, yous meritless, jeering, sneering throng——'

'He's lovely,' sighed Mrs. Brennan, 'like a mishing. Give the man a half, Michael. Go on now, Mr. Cripping. Tell us the poing. As poor ould Tom Moore said, "Carry on with the coffing, the corpse'll walk." '

'All right, so,' said Crippen, watching with a sneer Michael fill out the half; 'mind your hand doesn't slip. I suppose there'll be neither peace nor ease, nor any kind of good left me, barring I reveal my soul and my hurt to yous.'

'A bit of order now,' said Mrs. Brennan, 'and let the man show us his soul and his heart.'

Crippen lowered the half and projected his gaze far through Michael's window. Or to be precise, to the other side of East Arran Street, ten yards distant, the wall of the cabbage factory. He spoke in the agonized tones of one who had seen much, and didn't fancy any of it.

That's the way he spoke:

'There is a sadness in my sadness when I'm sad.
There is a gladness in my gladness when I'm glad.
There is a madness in my madness when I'm mad.
But the sadness in my sadness,
And the gladness in my gladness——'

'And the madness in your madness,' murmured Mrs. Brennan respectfully.

'—Are nothing to my badness when I'm bad.'

There was a moment's silence and Mrs. Brennan shook her head in the direction of the poet.

'Mr. Cripping,' she sighed, 'you're rotting. Rotting with braings.'

My great red racing bike

*

THIS WINTRY WEATHER reminds me of Dun Laoghaire.

Not, I hasten to add, that there's anything more wintry about the Dun than any place else this time of the year. The sea may lash up and over the East Pier, but then with my own two eyes I've seen the blue-clad Corporation employees of a famous Riviera town collecting newly fallen snow and throwing it into the Mediterranean. And a tourist nearly going in after it for trying to take a snapshot.

But when I was a young house-painting fellow of eight stone or so, and that's not today nor yesterday, taking one thing with another, weight for age, I was the possessor of a red racing bicycle called, if I remember rightly, a Phoenix, and inherited by me from my brother. His house-painting activity had taken him by train and car round the province of Connacht, from Boyle Cathedral to the Irish College in Tourmakeady, County Mayo.

He fell a total of more than a hundred feet in those two places, so his perambulations had something of the quality of a circus tour.

Of the bicycle I was very proud and a very skilful cyclist in traffic. I could get from the city to Dun Laoghaire while you'd be saying Lennox Robinson.

So when my employer wanted some stuff to be brought out to a job in the Borough, I took the tram fare but used the bicycle to get out there.

Which is how I came to have a shilling on a Tuesday.

It was the month of January and fairly cold in the morning but nothing exceptional about it, when I was starting off, but going through Ballsbridge it began spitting snow-water, and by the time I was at Blackrock the real genuine undiluted stuff was coming down in soft flakes, mild and gentle like a talk about Partition on the Third Programme. And by the time I got into Dun Laoghaire I was pushing through a blizzard.

The door of the house we were doing up was opened for me by an elderly painter, who was doing the job on his own. He was a native of the Channel Islands and went by the name of Janey.

I am not inventing this name. Poor Janey is no longer at this end of the plank, but I often wondered afterwards who did invent it. Maybe it was a corruption of his name in French.

'Come in, come in, young man, you are welcome,' said Janey. 'It's cold, isn't it?'

I shook myself like a whippet and admitted that it sure was, that you could play a melodeon to that.

'You 'ave terrible journey out to thees place,' said Janey. He always kept up a sort of a French fur-trapper's accent. The boss said that the old ones in the good-class trade liked it. I shook myself and nodded. 'You poor peeg,' said Janey.

Then after a minute or two he asked me, 'W'y you no come out in the . . . er . . . what you call tram-care?'

I told him I did not come out in the what-you-call-tram-care because I had a bike and wanted the shilling for myself. He nodded vigorously at this.

After we had a drop of tea and a bit of bread-and-brawn, Janey said it was no good my going back to the shop in that class of weather. I could get into stripping a room.

I went up to one of the upper rooms with stockbrush and scraper and set to work, but first I had to take up some linoleum.

This was a hazardous business for me. I never could resist reading old newspapers, and for me to raise a piece of old linoleum was like opening the door of a library.

I promised myself that I would only read a little bit, that I would just glance at the papers before I threw them into the snow outside, but when I raised the linoleum and saw the headline: 'Viceroy's visit to Grangegorman. Vicereine waves green linen handkerchief, scenes of mad enthusiasm,' I was lost and read it inch by inch, through the serial, 'Pretty Kitty'.

For new readers: 'Lord Maulverer has fallen in love with pretty Kitty Hackett, daughter of Honest Tom Hackett, a country butcher. She helps her father in the slaughter-house and one day she is busily gutting when an anxious moo is heard. . . .'

Till at last Janey came into the room and caught me there. The old English drop-pattern paper unscarred by hand of mine as I bent over the morning paper for Tuesday, 12th June 1901.

'So,' he moaned in his saddest Quebec accent. 'You 'ave down nowthing, no?'

'No,' said I, shamefaced.

'So,' said Janey. 'You are 'ere 'alf-day and you 'ave down nowthing. You come 'ere at 'alf-nine. That is right. On bicycle.' At this point his face increased. 'You 'ave mawnay?'

'That's right,' says I, 'I've a shilling.'

It seems Janey could do with the loan of a shilling: no sooner said than done. He went down the stairs with my shilling and I went back on my floor to my papers.

But I misjudged him, even though it was a deal from my point of view.

At half past two he came back and gave me five shillings. He was all smiles, but said, 'Now we do some graft; yes, no?' I agreed yes, no, it wouldn't kill us once in a way.

When we quit that night Janey told me he'd backed Pappegeno II, which won at a hundred-to-six—in a blizzard.

'In the boogies I did it. They 'ave boogies 'ere too,' said Janey. 'Jus' like 'ome in Daublin.'

To die without seeing
Dublin!

*

ONE OF THE Michael Dwyer crowd, whose breed still flourishes round New Street and thereabouts, was back on a visit from the Coombe to the Glen of Imaal, where his grandmother's sister lay dying.

After she was washed and made right for the road the priest sat taking a cup of tea and chatting with her. 'Well, now, and how do you feel, Nan?'

'I feel right enough, now that you've been and settled me; what would be the matter with me? I've known that I was going to die this eighty year past.

'It happened all belonging to me. Though them that does have all the talk about how nice it is in the next world, I don't see any great hurry on them getting on there.'

'I suppose you don't, Nan. But you've no regrets for this one. You reared fine men and women, and saw their rearing up here on the mountain.'

'I have no regret, Father, only the one. I was never in Dublin.'

Sammy Watt in Portrush has the same regret. In his youth there were no paid holidays and now, in ampler times, he's nervous that the Republicans would recognize him and have him shot, maybe lynch him as he walked along O'Connell Street, or tie him to the Bowl of Light place and, as a special Tóstal attraction, have him beaten to death with bound volumes of the *Ulster Protestant*.

For Sammy was on the other side in the Tan time.

176

I had never met anyone who boasted of having fought against the rebels, except the commissionaire of a Liverpool cinema who told me he was in the Black and Tans and took part in a military operation.

This included a raid on a clerical outfitter's in Dame Street.

Suitably garbed, he and his comrades, who had raided a pub or two earlier on, stood in the lorries and blessed the passers-by with upheld Mills grenades.

But the commissionaire only joined up because his girl friend wouldn't leave her work in a tripe factory. And, wanting to forget, he had not got the fare to the Foreign Legion and had to make do with the Black and Tans.

Besides, he thought it was more dangerous, the money was better, and he could help his widowed mother, who was an invalid and could do nothing but sit all day in a bathchair embroidering moral notices, suitable for framing, reading: 'Beware!'

'Just the one word,' said I, 'and the same one on all the notices?'

'Ah. She weren't much of a speller, my old woman. Nor much of an embroiderer, neither. She weren't bad though, considering the only training she'd ever 'ad was sewing mailbags when she'd be doing a couple of months up in Walton.

'She sent her embroidery all over the world with the missions. You could read "Beware" in my old woman's sewing all over the British Empire. Some places they didn't know enough English, and 'ad to 'ave it explained to them what it was about.

'When I was in your country, forgetting this judy what gave me up for a job in a tripe factory, my old woman, she sent me an embroidering, and it 'ung over the canteen counter—"Beware"—in black and red wool, till the shiners let off a landmine.

'It blew the roof in on top of the sergeant-major where 'e was 'avin' a pint, and when 'e got over 'is nerves, and got up and dusted 'imself, 'e said to take that so-and-so notice off the wall, or 'e'd go over to Norris Green and slit my old woman's gizzard, at 'is own expense.'

My commissionaire didn't count, because he wasn't much interested in the rights or wrongs of the war, so long as it kept his mind off his troubles.

Sammy spoke with the ardour of the pure-souled and dedicated patriot about his services to King and Empire in those strenuous days.

All my life I've known the opposite convention, where anyone old enough would mutter darkly about their doings, and if they weren't in the G.P.O. in 1916 it was because they were doing something more important, and to which the element of secrecy was so vital that it hasn't been made public nearly forty years after.

A change is as good as a rest.

'I'm a man that knows what I'm talking about. I was through the whole lot, so Ah was.'

'And what, pray, were you through?' asked his wife, from the far side of the table, 'barrin' it'd be a lock of porter barrels?'

'Och, hould your wheesht, you, Hanna, you knew nawthin' about it, nor was let know. A right thing, if every gabbin' ould woman in the County Derry could be knowing the secrets of the organization.'

'Och, what organization? Filling the wee boy's head up wi' your lies and rubbish.'

I signalled hastily to the barman.

'Port, please, for Mrs. Watt. No, not the Empire, the Portuguese port.'

It's not every day in these weeks I get called a 'wee boy'. It might never happen again.

'And a couple of scoops for myself and Sammy.'

We got settled down to his military reminiscences.

'Ah was an Intelligence man.'

'The dear God protect us from the Father of Lies,' muttered Hanna to herself, putting down her glass.

Sammy did not condescend to hear her. 'Yes, Ah was an undercover man like——'

'Dick Barton,' said Hanna.

'Ah was a spy, to tell you straight, though you were on the other side; good men on every side and you're a Fenian; you mind Dave O'Leary?' All in the one breath, and I had to sort it out as best I could.

Fenian Dave O'Leary?

'Would it be John O'Leary, Sammy? He was a Fenian, but he was in the one grave with romantic Ireland a long time before I was born.'

'Och, don't talk daft. This man was in the grave with no one. He stayed out in Portstewart, five mile out the town, only last summer. Isn't he the head one in the Free State? Damn it, sure everyone knows Dave O'Leary.'

'De Valera?'

'Damn it, isn't that who I said? Deyve Ah Leery.'

'Fair enough. What about him?'

'You mind the time he come in Columb's Hall in Derry? Well, Ah goes in, carryin' me life in me hands, among all these Fenians that's packin' the hall out, to give him a big cheer, when he comes out on the stage to prache.'

'To?'

'To prache the meeting. Ah'm sitting in the sate minding no one and hoping no one will mind me, but I'm in me disguise.'

'What was that,' asked Hanna, 'a temperance pin?'

'I took me hat off, and no one in the place had ever seen the top of me head from the time I got bald, so they didn't know me.

'Till, when Dave O'Leary comes out on the stage there's a big cheer, and a roar, and the next thing is, the peelers is trying to get in the doors and the crowd is baiting them, and Dave O'Leary is away there, up on the stage, and he says that he came to prache, and, begor, he's going to prache, and damn the one will stop him, and in the middle of it I've got down under the seat, and Head Constable Simpson says, "Got you," and he doesn't know me with me bald head till he turns me round and recognizes me from me face, and near drops from surprise.

' "And what and under the dear good God are you doing here, Sammy Watt? D'you think we hadn't enough trouble with the Fenians?"

' "Ah'm an Intelligence man," said I. "A spy."

' "Take yourself to hell out of thon, or I'll spy you, with a kick, where it won't blind you." There was me thanks.'

'Ah, sure wasn't it always the way. Look at Parnell.'

'Ah wonder would they hould it again me in Dublin if I snaked down for a wee trip on the *Enterprise*?'

'Couldn't you disguise yourself? Take off your hat until you get back on the train?'

Yes, quare times

*

AT NAAS RACES I wondered why the chalk fell from the bookies' paralysed paws when they came to the name of Quare Times.

Being an eager seeker after information about anything except picks and shovels, I decided to ask a bookie why this was. I looked round and, though I have been acquainted with some of them since childhood, there was a forbidding look of foreboding about them all that did not invite enquiries as to the cause of their worries. Except Rory Curran, whose bland and pleasant smile swept round the multitude, like a beam of a lighthouse on a dark and troubled sea. I went over, stood under, and looked up at him.

'Rory, a chara.'

'Just a moment, Brendan, till I'm done with this gentleman.'

He muttered something about four score and ten to his clerk, though whether it referred to your gills's age or not I do not know, though they threw the old man's tenners in the bag, as if they were sure they were to stay there, and asked of me, 'How's the form?'

'Very good,' said I, 'as a matter of fact, if I was better I couldn't stick it.'

'More of that to you. Are you having a small punt?'

'It would not be right for me to bet you sixty pound to forty pound that this horse will be first past the post. I'm not the bookmaker.'

'And maybe you haven't got the sixty pound,' said the clerk.

'Oh, he'd have it about him all right,' said Rory.

'I suppose you could be right,' said the clerk, measuring the front of my overcoat and muttering something about taking more exercise.

An aged turf accountant who whenever I pass usually takes care to flash the far side of his bag, where it reads, 'Mimimum Bet 2/-', looked at me with a new interest. I may say the near side of the bag reads, 'Jack Kennedy, Baa, Tonafarraga', which I believe is in the County Belcuddy or some such place.

Anyway, the punters would have a right time trying to catch up to *him* in his native warren. And even if you did there's no knowing whether they come under Dev's dominion at all or not.

A small, red-faced man with the figure of a ferret, nodded knowingly, as he has a habit of doing. This person, like the character in Dostoyevsky's *The Idiot*, was a man who brought the art of knowing other people's business to the level of a science, and I heard him telling the true story of the Tóstal, the behind-hand work that went on about the Shannon Scheme, and who worked the oracle in the case of the nine million sods of turf at Co. Meath—wheels within wheels, and it's not what you know but who you know—have you me?

In answer to my query re the bookies' reaction to Quare Times—which was worse than the panic aboard the Liverpool boat one trip they ran out of porter and wanted the people to drink milk stout—Rory told me to go round and have a look at the animal going round the parade ring.

Which I did, and I might as well have been a sow looking into a swill barrel for all the good it did me.

Quare Times looked a magnificent beast, but I suppose it's because of long years of running with dockets from building jobs in the light and *aerach*[1] days of my youth have conditioned me to thinking that racing is all an affair of telephones and duplicated sheets, and old ones with string bags saying they

[1] Carefree.

got it off a man off a boat or a train, or latterly an Aer Lingus plane, so that if you wanted to make sure of the Spring Double, by considerations of distance, you'd want to get hold of a man from Mars.

But my walk was not entirely wasted, because I heard two ladies talking about a hunt to an old fellow with a bowler hat, drain-pipe trousers, nap coat with a velvet collar.

One of the ladies put her teeth up in an elegant snarl and said to this old Teddy Boy: 'Well, m'lard, he's paffectly impossible as an Emmeffaitch.[1] Only wants the Cambridge Drag.'

The old lard was got up for the Creep, but he only said, 'Emahdone-noe, but he might finish up as the most popular Emmeffaitch they've ever had, better than the last and most frightful creature, pots of money, no breeding, shouting— instead of "Tally-ho"—"Come on, after the ——" '

I got back and described these happenings to Rory just before the off.

[1] Master of Foxhounds.

Ferret-face nodded, though no one had asked him, and told us who m'lard was.

I was going off when I heard him make reference to myself.

'He's a professional Unionist. Very cultured class of a chap, too; writes a rubber cheque, in Irish.'

I turned round and said, 'Only on St. Patrick's Day,' and fled up the stand before I'd hear my true history.

Shake hands with an Alsatian

*

I WISH YOU ALL a happy St. Patrick's Day and that you may not go entirely short of provisions is the sincere wish of me and mine to you and yours. (You can be fairly certain that I won't—not if I have to shake paws with half the Alsatians in the country.)

Talking about Alsatians—you can knock off those brackets. I don't know what I put them up there for, only to be literary—they are not my favourite animal. I was related to an Alsatian by marriage. Wolf was his name, and he barked his head off any time I put my head in my first wife's family's door.

They always reassured me that he meant well, and that his bark was worse than his bite, but that could easy mean that his bite could be bad enough.

In any event, if he got away with a good lump of me it would not be much good running after him to get it back. He was at least a 30-50 dog.

I like little dogs like Pomeramanses or Petingeeses, but my favourite show animal is Anna Kelly's famous cat Groucho.

He has the longest whiskers in Catland, and I think should be more properly called Salvador Dali, after the painter, who maintains that his extra-long whiskers are the wireless aerials of his soul.

I'm not sure that my favourite animal, taken one way or another, is not Mr. M. Cash's 'Umindme' b.g. by Umidkhan, which did me a great obligement at Two-Mile-House Point-to-Point on Tuesday. But, anyway, poor old Wolf, my

Alsatian-in-law, is now croaked, and *de mortuis nil nisi bom
bom*, as they used to teach us in the Latin class in my old
school.

The happiest animal I have seen is the greyhound Spanish
Battleship, and I must say that he even seemed to put his
connections into good humour, when all is said and done.

My grandmother had an enormous cat that went by the
name of Beeshams. I can only describe it by saying that his
father's name was Lynchehaun, and it looked every inch a son
of its father.

It was a rather outstanding animal, by reason of the fact that
it seemed to enjoy white snuff. Be damn, but that's a thing you
don't often meet with in a cat, but it was the truth about
Beeshams.

My granny had it rest upon her bosom, with his two front
paws round her neck and his fat old head wagging from side

to side with every intonation of her voice, as if he knew what she was saying.

His two eyes fixed on hers, as if she was Sir Anthony Eden and he was a licensed grocer from Bangor, Co. Down, hoping to be mentioned in the New Year's Honours List.

White snuff fell generously about her person, but Beeshams did not mind. He even sniffed the snuff, and wrinkled his chops as if he liked it.

'Me poor lanna walla,' my granny would say, under the impression that she was speaking to the beast in the Irish language.

Her ideas of that tongue were of the sketchiest, but her heart was good, and she usually addressed Beeshams in Irish for a go-off, as she maintained that only he understood her dialect.

'Me poor lanna walla,' she'd croon, and the old cat would wag his head slowly, 'sure it's the queer drisheen I'd be after begrudging you,' upon which she would produce a piece of Herr Youkstetter's good old Irish black pudding, and this happened regularly, though Beeshams was restricted to Sundays and Patrick's Day in Lent.

'Beeshams bucked,' she would moan. 'I might as well be boss in Erin if it wasn't for you, me good old bruteen.'

'What's a bruteen?' I asked her.

'A bruteen is a little cat.'

'It's no such a thing,' said I, 'being in fifth class and knowing all about *Algebair*[1] and *Teagasc Criostai*[2] *agus an Atlantach Thuaidh*[3] *agus an Tuiseal Geineamhnach Uimhir Iolraidh.*[4] I should know.'

'You're an impudent cur to downface your own granny.'

'A little cat is *"cat beag".*'

'You caught no bug in this house barring you brought it in with you,' and she spoke into Beeshams's old face. 'Oh, culla

---

[1] Algebra.
[2] Christian Doctrine (the catechism).
[3] North Atlantic.
[4] Possessive case plural number.

culla, no luck.' Then she turned to me and said, 'I suppose you have the brass impertinence to tell me that "No luck" does not mean "no mice"?' And Beeshams would give a deep purr and she'd answer, 'Ah-ha, colleen bawn.'

'And if it goes to that, it should be *buachaill ban*. Beeshams is a he-cat,' I said.

'You mind your own business, me little man cut short,' she said. 'Beeshams is not asking you what he is,' and she directed her gaze into the cat's face. 'Ah, bah, carrageen?'

Sermons in cats, dogs—
and mice

*

THERE IS a collection of essays in the Penguin series called *Music At Night*. They were written by Aldous Huxley about twenty years ago. Although a Penguin-educated citizen myself, I read this book a lot of years ago before it was in Penguins, at a time when I was leading a more contemplative life and had plenty of time to think about what I read.

One of the essays deals with the next world, and what we are likely to be doing in it, and is called *Squeak and Gibber*.

I was thinking of the essay Huxley calls *Sermons in Cats*.

A man wishing to be a writer wants Huxley to tell him the best way to go about it. Now don't think I'm going to set up in an advisory capacity on this matter.

Seán O Faoláin, father confessor, nursemaid, and prison visitor to some of my grade, used to say that the equipment of a writer should consist of pen, paper, and a time-sheet. To write, and see that you wrote a certain amount every day. And a ledger to note what you sent out in the way of MSS. and what you got for them.

Huxley advises your man to watch cats. They live and love, are jealous, mean, generous, and all to that effect.

He says that the man to whom he gave this advice did not seem very grateful for it.

I'd have picked up a cat and hit him a belt of it. Only I happen to like cats.

For his advice was rubbishy, and there is nothing about

human beings that cannot be learned better from human beings than from any other creature that lives on earth.

The man who said that the more he saw of mankind, the more he liked his dog, was some species of informer or handman's labourer, that his own mother would run away from, could she but lose him in a big enough crowd.

And the dog was the leavings of a lurcher that only stopped with him because he was too weak with the hunger for his legs to carry him any more than two yards in the one day.

'I'll never forget our poor ould bowler,' said Mrs. Brennan. 'Poor ould Pram. Poor faithful ould K-mine.'

'What's mine?'

'K-mine. I don't like calling him a brute. I know they've no souls, but you never know what he might be in another world listening to us. Not but what,' she added, significantly, 'but what they might be as well entitled to souls as certain individgeyoulums I know.'

'That'll do you now,' said Crippen. 'None of your theology. This is a respectable house.'

Mrs. Brennan, lost in mournful recollection, sighed, 'Ah, poor ould Pram.'

'Pram?' said I.

'That's right. We called him "Pram" after the dog that belonged to Fill Mac Coon.'[1]

Cats are not know-alls. They are independent enough, and nobody ever saw a cat at one end of a lead and a policeman at the other. Belloc says they are of the breed of the devil and cannot be poisoned. Too often this has been disproved.

People (for some reason of the would-be yokel variety) like to hang their tongues, village-idiot fashion, and tell you how they cannot stick cats.

'Well,' my mother's first mother-in-law would say, 'd'you prefer rats?'

Leaving that to one side, cats have their rights as well as anyone under the constitution of this State, and it's a punishable

[1] Finn Mac Cool: legendary Irish hero.

offence to put them into areas in the new converted Corporation flats, so that they're trapped and die of starvation and thirst after days of agony.

The older people in those parts know that only for the cats we'd never have survived in those rat-warrens. Children growing up in better times may not realize this.

That is the point of this sermon. And if they don't they take it to heart, I know certain little devils that will be getting a kick where it won't blind them.

The late Sister Monica, who taught generations of boys, including Sean Russell, and one of the editors of the *Irish Digest*, and the present writer, at North William Street School, was encouraging a boy called Champers, who, even for that district, was considered a chaw of some dimensions. Some

doubted whether he was a human being at all, and by his shaggy looks and his taste for raw vegetables and chewing tobacco he might have escaped from a circus.

Champers, by dint of much pen-chewing, finally produced a composition: *The Autobiography of a Mouse.*

'I was a muss. So was me mother and me father and we all et chees till the cat kem an et me da an me ma an me an all.'

'Now, Stanislaus Kostka'—this was Champers' real name—'that is really very good indeed and most interesting, but,' and Sister Monica looked at him earnestly from under her big linen bonnet, 'if the mouse was eaten by the cat, how could he have written his autobiography?'

Champers looked at her scornfully, and asked with great patience, 'Listen, Sister, how could a mouse write his beeyog-rafee anyway?'